THERE'S GOT TO BE A BETTER WAY

AN OVERACHIEVER'S GUIDE TO DISCOVERING JOY

KAREN PERY

This is a work of nonfiction. Any resemblance to persons living or dead should be plainly apparent to them and those who know them, especially if the author has been kind enough to have provided their real names and, in some cases, their endearing pet names. All events described herein are all true from the author's perspective, with some of the details adjusted to protect client confidentiality, some lost over time, and some recrafted to consolidate timelines.

The content of this book is for general instruction only. Each person's physical, emotional, and spiritual condition is unique. The instruction in this book is not intended to replace or interrupt the reader's relationship with a physician or other mental health professional. Please consult your doctor for matters pertaining to your specific health.

Copyright © 2019 by Karen Pery

All rights reserved.

Printed in the United States of America.

Editing by Amanda Johnson, Awaken Village Press
Cover design by Melissa Stone
Cover photography by Seth Murray, elementz photography
Interior design by Caitlin Pisha

ISBN 978-0-578-40399-1 (paperback)
ISBN 978-0-578-40400-4 (ebook)

Library of Congress Control Number: 2018962321

Published by Awaken Village Press
www.awakenvillagepress.com

THERE'S GOT TO BE A BETTER WAY

AN OVERACHIEVER'S GUIDE TO DISCOVERING JOY

KAREN PERY

AWAKEN VILLAGE PRESS

PRAISE FOR
THERE'S GOT TO BE A BETTER WAY

Karen is a longtime friend and fellow executive coach. Her writing reminds me of sitting next to her in the countryside in the shade of a beautiful tree with a glass of lemonade, as we talk about the things that matter to us most: family, healing, work, love, wonder, curiosity, and vulnerability. If you've not had the chance to sit next to her and share stories in the sunshine, this book is the next best thing.

**MARCY SWENSON,
CO-FOUNDER STARTUP HAPPINESS,
PARTNER TEST KITCHEN CAPITAL**

A wise and intimate must-read for every individual who yearns to create their biggest, boldest life and is open to some very smart reflections and suggestions. This book takes the reader on an intimate and candid adventure of the spirit—through loss, love, and laughter—reminding each of us that unfolding before us is a better way to live our biggest life.

LINDA MOORE,
FOUNDER & ADVISOR, TNG

Karen is a consummate storyteller; her stories have stories. *There's Got to Be a Better Way* comes complete with excellent adventures like giving a presentation while completing a ropes course, leading surf retreats in Hawaii, and learning and teaching leadership with horses. Karen takes you on a journey into the intimate and tender adventures of her life with hopes that you can learn more about yours. She has navigated real and hard things like recovering from perfectionism, trauma, and grief. She is a generous and fun overachiever that has done a lot of the work for you so, just maybe, you don't have to do it for yourself. But if you do find that you have to do your own hard work, she will help you realize that you aren't alone. Karen takes on marriage, parenting, unexpectedly intimate relationships, unexpressed faith, constant reinvention, and poignant loss. Karen will help you more clearly understand your own journey and inspire you to take the leap into what's next for you. Welcome to the adventure.

CARRIE KISH,
CEO, CULTURESYNC

This is not your mother's self-help book. With a sense of humor and filled with emotional highs and lows, *There's Got to Be a Better Way* takes you on an excellent adventure through trauma, healing, career, and motherhood offering tools and stories to help you find your own better way. As someone who's tried to "hack" my way into self-help to achieve balance, this book is an essential guide!

ANDREA OWEN,
LIFE COACH AND AUTHOR OF
*HOW TO STOP FEELING LIKE SH*T*
AND *52 WAYS TO LIVE
A KICK ASS LIFE*

There's Got to Be a Better Way charms and challenges the reader to experience the mundane in the cosmic, the glorious in the mundane, and ultimately encourages a deep appreciation for the simple moments, within which lie the potential for deep fulfillment and personal transformation.

CHRIS CHARYK,
EXECUTIVE COACH,
THE BODA GROUP

If there was ever someone who loved to make things *not easy* but did so with the biggest heart on this planet…it's Karen. In her search for truth, beauty, perfection, synergy, and goodness, she somehow was able to place herself dead last in her life a lot of the time. I have a sneaking suspicion this is why her book is titled *There's Got to Be a Better Way*; that and because she was always trying to find it.

As luck, fate, and/or the universe would have it, Karen gave herself the biggest gift of all. She fell in love with who she is unconditionally. In doing so, this book was nurtured into being, and the world gets to enjoy the presence and wisdom that comes from LOVE. Unconditional love.

I've been fortunate enough to know Karen through the highs and lows of her recent life. The first things I saw in Karen were her optimism and joy: I felt vividly her desire to serve, teach, and help and make it fun, adventurous, and somehow peaceful. Through it all, she kept coming back home to her heart. This book is a gift to you, the reader, as a means for you to find your way back home to your heart, to loving the stranger that is yourself, as Walcott beautifully writes.

In doing so you, too, can find a better way. Your own better way. What a gift.

GARY MAHLER,
EXECUTIVE COACH,
CO-FOUNDER INTO THE FIRE LEADERSHIP

There's Got To Be A Better Way reminds each of us that there is a better way when it comes to transforming our life experiences into opportunities to awaken our spirit. Karen pours every bit of her big heart and generous soul into each page of this masterpiece. You will be touched, moved, and inspired by the brilliance and authenticity of her story.

**DEVON BANDISON,
EXECUTIVE COACH AND AUTHOR OF
*FATHERHOOD IS LEADERSHIP***

A must-read for every person who wants to learn about empathy, compassion, self-love, and the ingredients required to heal, flourish, and grow on this journey we call "life."

**CAROLYN DUCKWORTH,
SENIOR BUSINESS PARTNER,
EXPERIENCEPOINT**

CONTENTS

1	WINDOWS TO MY SOUL
3	THIS IS NOT AN INSTRUCTION MANUAL
8	LEADERSHIP: A LOVE LETTER
10	INNER CHILD AGAIN
11	SENSITIVE
15	TRAUMA BRAIN
19	RESEARCHING LIFE
20	TIPS FOR BEING POWERFUL AND SENSITIVE
24	WEIRD IS GOOD
26	A LETTER FROM MY FUTURE SELF
29	WORKING GIRL
32	A LIST OF THINGS CAPTURED IN A MOMENT
35	KAREN THE COLLEGE APPLICANT
39	MAJORING IN LIFE
42	FAILURE *IS* AN OPTION
46	REALITY BITES
50	INTUITION, TAKE THE WHEEL

52	BABY STEPS
56	WORK 10, LIFE 3
59	INTUITION LOOKS LIKE THIS TO ME
61	PREPARING TO FALL IN LOVE AGAIN
63	THANK YOU, OPRAH.
65	I'M FREE
68	DATING 101
70	IT WAS A DARK AND STORMY NIGHT…
73	HORSE REFLECTIONS: A CONVERSATION BETWEEN RAFE AND KAREN
76	THE ONE
78	IT ALL HAPPENED SO FAST
80	THE CRASH OF 2002
83	INSIDE OUTSIDE, UPSIDE DOWN
86	EXCELLENT ADVENTURES: A CONVERSATION BETWEEN RAFE AND KAREN
89	ALL ABOUT MY MOTHER
93	I INVENTED MOTHERHOOD
96	MOTHERHOOD REINVENTED
98	THE RIGHT WAY TO PARENT
101	BEGIN AGAIN

104	SWEET LITTLE GIRL
106	ACCOMPLISHMENT JUNKIE
110	MORE THAN "JUST A MOM"
116	THE UNSUNG HERO
118	MISS INDEPENDENT
122	"WIGGLE YOUR BUTT!"
126	MARTYR MOM IS IN THE HOUSE
129	COMING TOGETHER AND FALLING APART
131	MIRROR, MIRROR
132	WHOA!
135	HOW TO TAKE CARE OF ME, BY ME
140	COACHING: A CONVERSATION BETWEEN RAFE AND KAREN
142	NO ONE TOLD ME
144	AN OPTIMIST FOR EVERYONE ELSE
145	UNWRITTEN
147	UNWRITTEN (CONTINUED)
148	LOST IN TRANSLATION
151	EQUINE EMPOWERMENT
155	DESERVING
157	THE FOG

160	UNLIKELY PAIR
164	THIS IS WHAT IT LOOKS LIKE… WHEN I AM FALLING APART
168	ACCOMPLISHMENT JUNKIE, PART 2
171	FLEUR DE SEL CARAMEL, MY MARE, MY MIRROR
174	HOPES & DREAMS
177	EXCELLENT ADVENTURES: A CONVERSATION BETWEEN RAFE AND KAREN (CONTINUED)
180	I'LL DO ANYTHING
183	WHAT I KNOW ABOUT THE PAST, PRESENT, AND FUTURE
185	THE LOOK
188	THE BIRTH OF INTO THE FIRE
193	THE SIZE OF MY WORLD
195	EXCELLENT ADVENTURES: A CONVERSATION BETWEEN RAFE AND KAREN (CONTINUED)
198	WONDER TWINS
202	HELP WANTED
205	CHOOSING LOVE OVER FEAR
207	CON(FIDENCE) WOMAN
210	#32 ON MY BUCKET LIST: LEARN TO SURF
215	WHEN ONE DOOR CLOSES…
218	STAY STOKED

221	THE LIST, PART 2
224	GOOD LUCK, GIDGET.
227	LOWENSTEIN
231	THE SPIRITUAL MECHANIC
235	DYING INSIDE?
237	DYING INSIDE: A CONVERSATION BETWEEN RAFE AND KAREN
240	TRAUMA BRAIN, PART 2
244	BORN TO LOVE
248	WAVES BREAK
252	WAKE-UP WEDNESDAY
255	NO REQUESTS ARE OFF LIMITS
259	ZUMA MEANS ABUNDANCE
262	LIFE LESSONS FROM A SEPHORA MAKEOVER
265	LET'S COLOR AND GO IN THE OCEAN
267	TRAUMA BRAIN, PART 3
270	HOME
272	MY VILLAGE: ACKNOWLEDGMENTS
274	RESOURCES
277	ABOUT THE AUTHOR

WINDOWS TO MY SOUL

IF AT THE END OF MY DAYS I saw my life flashing before my eyes, these windows to my soul would create some of the most moving and memorable moments of the film.

(1)   Standing together on the balcony of a South Beach, Florida hotel one hot August night watching thunderstorms roll through the sky.

(2)   Walking around the gardens of the county museum of art, knowing I could not let the day end without telling him *I love you*.

(3)   My eyes scrolling down the typed list taped inside the window of the high school activities office announcing newly appointed officers to student government and seeing my name.

(4)   My hand against the cool worn stones on the wall in Jerusalem, seeing the messages people had tucked in its crevices, knowing I wished for nothing, that all I had was all I would ever need.

(5)   The view of the lights along the Champs-Élysées from atop the Arc de Triomphe—a place I'd only seen in high school French class videos, imagining myself there while looking at the poster taped to the back of my bedroom door—after climbing all 284 stairs to the top in the rain late at night prior to closing insisting we should because *when was the next time we would be in Paris?*

(6) Alone with my newborn son in the dimly lit hospital room, stretching out his tiny fingers against mine as I told him the stories of our family so he would know who he would be meeting and how very loved he already was.

(7) His face as I walked down the aisle.

(8) My hand on her mane in the waning sunlight of an autumn afternoon, touching the glistening golden brown locks, hearing in my mind *she'll be called Fleur because she is the color of a Fleur de Sel caramel.*

(9) Leaving the ultrasound, walking across the street to a department store and buying her very first pink dress.

(10) Surfing a long, slow, right curling wave off Waikiki Beach, seeing Diamond Head in the distance one way, my family on the beach the other, and feeling *this is the stuff of dreams.*

THIS IS NOT AN INSTRUCTION MANUAL

IF YOU'RE LOOKING FOR a prescription or routine that will help you feel better starting right now, I suggest you go outside and take a walk.

No one has it figured out. We're all doing our best and making it up as we go along.

There is not one way to live your best life. The key word in this sentence is *your*. You are the most important person in the world because you are YOU.

What we do does not make us successful. To borrow unapologetically from Prince, you don't have to be rich, you don't have to be cool, you don't have to be beautiful. What is success but to live life on your terms according to what matters to you? Until you define it for yourself, success means nothing.

The words that follow were written from 2003 through the spring of 2018. It's a collection of stories that took place over time—some written while I was in the thick of it, others as a reflection of what I learned, written for different audiences, some just for myself. This book weaves together the journey of who I thought I was *supposed* to be with who I really am.

Writing was a way to pause and reflect while everything and everyone around me was changing. I wrote in journals, in a mom's group newsletter while serving multiple terms as president, and on my personal blog.

If I wrote something that impacted someone, it was mostly unintentional. I wrote with an inauthentic anonymity, known publicly as "jakelliesmom." It was yet another label I applied to myself, a reduction of my identity into the role I was currently serving. I'd been many things to many people: a good girl, a straight A student, a girlfriend, a scholar. When I wrote, I found a voice I didn't know I had—not an identity but rather a window to my soul.

With a deeper connection to myself, telling the truth of my life and not the picture-perfect image I tried desperately to maintain when everything around me was chaos, I was free to live, breathe, and just *be me*. I was honest.

I look back not to go back, but to honor who I was becoming in the telling of my heroic journey. I witness myself through windows of knowing. I see myself emerge from the twisted path from there to here.

The stories I share are all true from my perspective with some of the details adjusted to protect client confidentiality, some lost over time, and some recrafted to consolidate timelines.

I neither believe that hindsight is 20/20 nor that time heals all wounds, but like silver, sometimes a bit of tarnish or polish improves it. It's my heartfelt intention to be as real, raw, and true as possible, knowing that some of the material may be sensitive and triggering to some of you. It certainly has been to me. Perspective is complex, multi-dimensional, and tricky because it's ever changing, just like us.

As much as I have struggled to say it, I am both inspiring and successful. I have overcome trauma that has left deep and lasting scars. I have constructed and deconstructed myself more times than I can count. I have created and witnessed miracles. I love myself with my whole heart. None of this is particularly easy for me to say out loud for an old fear of being judged, but I know no one could ever judge me as harshly as I once judged myself. Fear can be unkind.

Some of the most powerful work I've ever done is writing what feels most vulnerable to reveal, what's hardest to say out loud. Writing is a solitary pursuit that makes me feel less alone. I write because, when I do, I connect to other people. I am a conduit for shared experiences made visible because I've opened the curtains to a window of my life. I write because I have to. If I don't give them a place to live, the words, phrases, and ideas will haunt me. Once they are planted in a story, they are turned over and cultivated. They become the fertile, nutrient soil that grows new ideas and changes what is possible.

As I've sat with my stories, some never before shared, I have asked myself *why this* and *why now*?

Part of me says, it's time to let these stories go into the world to live on their own. Another part of me says, I'm writing this to heal and release the past so I can fully and joyfully live in the present. Then, there is this persistent, loud voice inside me that bellows: IF ONE PERSON READS THIS BOOK AND IMAGINES A BETTER WAY TO LIVE THEIR LIFE, IT WILL BE WORTH IT.

That's my inner voice. It's powerful and comes straight from my heart. It took me many years to learn to listen to, trust, and, better yet, *love* the sound of it. My inner voice—some would call it intuition or gut instinct or voice of God or a sixth sense—has guided me to live the most magical life. I found joy when I learned to follow the wisdom of my internal GPS. It has been my guiding light, my personal North Star, and led me to start my own business, save my marriage, climb trees, surf, learn to dance, and listen to the whispers of horses and help others do the same.

Whatever you want to call it, I believe we are universally equipped with innate wisdom. For some of us, it is highly cultivated, and we can live, work, and create in flow. For others, it may seem like your inner voice speaks in a foreign tongue. My goal in sharing my stories is to help you bridge the gap between who you think you're *supposed* to be and knowing who you *truly* are by learning to discover and love your inner voice so that you, too, can be free to enjoy your life exactly as it is and exactly as YOU are.

I found the better way, and I was stunned: my life is so much better than I ever dreamed it could be.

> *Two roads diverged in a wood, and I—*
>
> *I took the one less traveled by,*
>
> *And that has made all the difference.*
>
> *– Robert Frost*

LEADERSHIP: A LOVE LETTER

WHEN I WAS A LITTLE GIRL, I spent hours reading, imagining myself solving mysteries like Nancy Drew or taking care of a horse like in *Black Beauty*. I went for long walks alone and with my friends, and I planned out my life—I'd be a lawyer at twenty-five, married, then a mom with a boy and a girl.

I first learned that I could change the future when I was 11. My friend campaigned to be our elementary school's elected vice president, and I served as her manager. Though we lost the election, a spark was ignited. The idea of serving our school was exciting to me, a newcomer who wanted to belong and saw opportunities to make the world of Valencia Elementary a better place. Leadership has always been my second language. I listen to what the people around me want and need, and together we create a vision of what can be.

I never stopped following this path, though at times my flame was nearly out, especially in the dark years between when I decided not to become an attorney and before I became mom to my son and daughter. In exchange for a career, I'd given away pieces of myself until I was almost unrecognizable.

Like my teenage detective alter ego, I began looking at the clues from my past to rekindle my life in a new way. A cultivated ability to listen made me an excellent coach, and I began working with individuals and organizations to build their new and improved future.

What about my future? In 2011, I was at a crossroads. A few years into my first true entrepreneurial journey (since I didn't consider babysitting and selling our family chickens' eggs to the neighbors as businesses), I was frustrated, bored, and discouraged. My inner fire was flickering and weak. My husband and I, both business owners, fell into a joyless grind of parenting and work. It was relentless. There had to be a better way.

Within a year, I began discovering my better way. I could not have been more surprised—how it looked, felt, and occurred. It was so much easier than I'd thought.

INNER CHILD AGAIN

WHAT WOULD YOUR INNER CHILD SAY *to you now as you offer her unconditional love, support, and acceptance, what she always longed for?*

As I heard the psychologist ask me a question I've been asked way too many times, I had to stop my inner teenager's eyes from rolling.

It was different this time.

Closing my eyes, I could picture my inner preschooler hard at work. Hearing the question, sighing, looking up from her project with a hardened gaze, saying out loud, "Prove it."

And what would you do? How would you respond?

"I'd smile at her and keep showing up," I tell him. "I'd wear her down with love. I'm persistent. Eventually, she'll know I mean it."

And then?

"Then it will be okay."

SENSITIVE

EVEN BEFORE MY DADDY DIED when I was four, I was a sensitive and hyper-aware child. I was keenly attuned to what the adults around me felt, thought, needed, and expected—especially my mom who was often angry, which I learned to accept but never understood and did everything I could to avoid. I was able to read others and adapt my behavior to fit in and be accepted and loved.

Dr. Judith Orloff's description of what it feels like to be an empath nails it for me:

> *We are so sensitive that it's like holding something in a hand that has fifty fingers instead of five. We are truly super responders.*

In preschool, at the age of two, I stood outside my classroom and overheard two moms commenting on one child's artwork in the hall. "It looks like a ballerina," one said, and I remember thinking *it looks like a bunch of scribbles*. But I wanted their approval and, had I the talent, I would have drawn ballerina scribbles, too. Another mom once said I'd be beautiful like her if I ate the crusts of my bread, so, even though she wasn't beautiful to me, I ate the tasteless crusts of peanut butter and jelly because it was expected, and approval meant belonging. I overheard parents speaking of how many paper towels we were supposed to use in the restroom, and I deliberately used only half of a sheet knowing I'd be praised as a model citizen.

It is a tremendous amount of responsibility for a toddler to anticipate what the adults around need in order to feel a sense of security, period. But it got worse from there.

Losing a parent at any age is difficult. Losing my Daddy, my hero, the most wonderful being in the Universe, made no sense to me.

It was an accident. He left our home in the evening to go to night school, and within the hour he was gone, killed instantly when he and his motorcycle made impact with another vehicle.

I remember the night of his accident with excruciating detail. The faded harvest gold wall-mounted rotary phone ringing as the summer sun was setting the night of July 3, 1975. Mom dropping us off at a neighbor's house with kids my brother knew from Cub Scouts. *The Three Stooges* playing on a TV set in black and white. Hearing the older kids asking out loud if we thought my dad was dead and feeling judged for laughing when everyone else was worried and scared even though *The Three Stooges* wasn't funny to me, but sometimes it was. Being up after midnight when Mom came home from the emergency room with my brother Ryan, then eight, and my mom's best friend Shirley and her husband, Doug. Everyone was sobbing, but I couldn't cry. I wondered if Daddy had died because Ryan made dessert that night? I thought Ryan was crying because he wouldn't get to look at motorcycles with Daddy on the weekend like they'd planned.

That story is easy to tell, unlike some others.

I would never tell you the stories that have haunted me since of how my mom managed as a single parent and how she raised us after my Daddy was gone. Memories and moments of the worst days have cycled through my mind as flashbacks, looping on repeat, my whole life.

I would tell you that my mom did her best but never how anxious or afraid I was or what she did that made me afraid. The mother I remember from my childhood was absent at best. I had no idea that she was depressed.

From that point forward, life was unpredictable. There was always a moving target. The very worst thing in the world had just happened. But life went on, and we were a new family now without my Daddy.

One evening, my mom was boiling water for corn on the cob. She asked me to take the cat outside so we could eat, and as I was getting the cat, my mom tripped over us, spilling scalding hot water all over my back.

We rushed to the emergency room (I imagine the same one where my Daddy was taken after his accident), and I sat alone on a gurney, my mom outside in the waiting room with my brother. It felt like everyone and everything else was more important than me, even the chats around the coffee maker in the nurses' station. I watched it all happening.

I wasn't so much scared as I was lonely. Nothing hurt, but I had to cry to get someone to pay attention to me. It is one of the first times I remember having to do more or extra—basically adapting my behavior or action—for someone to notice me. They did, and I got what I wanted—at least on the surface. What I really wanted was for my Daddy to hold me and tell me it would be okay, but he couldn't. He was gone. I wanted my mom to love me and understand me and see how hurt and scared I was, instead of strong and resilient, which is who I'd become because that's who I believed she needed me to be.

From that moment on, I became who I thought I was supposed to be and did what I needed to do in order to be loved and accepted by everyone in my life, starting with my mom. I developed strategies to: 1) avoid her rage and 2) not need her (or anyone else) to take care of me. This was my best attempt to protect myself from ever feeling hurt again. I never wanted to have to depend on *anyone* because anyone can die and leave you. If I could rely on myself, I would be safe.

I would never tell you how often I've woken up in terror from dreams that are so vivid and real I feel helpless. I cannot scream because I have no voice. Why would I ever tell you this? On the outside, I look like I have it all together. It is so much easier to look good and keep up the clever disguise than to face the hard facts: I am a survivor of childhood trauma, abuse, and neglect.

TRAUMA BRAIN

I'VE BEEN A GROWN-UP FOR a very long time and wasn't willing to admit I had a problem. I never had a rock bottom and didn't know I needed help until one day, when it occurred to me that the people around me who were flourishing weren't always looking to the past for answers. I bet they didn't constantly have flashbacks and nightmares, either.

I never talked about it, not to my husband, not to my best friends. I couldn't. I assumed everyone had their "stuff," and I prided myself on my resilience and how much I had accomplished and overcome on my own despite my circumstances.

But I remembered something Dr. Brené Brown wrote about shame:

> *Shame needs three things to grow out of control in our lives: secrecy, silence and judgment. When something shaming happens and we keep it locked up, it festers and grows. It consumes us. We need to share our experiences. Shame happens between people, and it heals between people.* ***If we can find someone who has earned the right to hear our story, we need to tell it.*** (Gifts of Imperfection, page 40)

On the one hand, I was proud of who I'd become and what I'd done; on the other, I was deeply ashamed that my trauma was what motivated me.

Around the time I realized my backward thinking might be flawed and that flashbacks and nightmares were not the norm, I heard a podcast with Tim Ferriss featuring Dr. Gabor Maté focusing on addiction that mentioned trauma and sensitivity. I didn't have addiction, but I certainly had the other two. I listened once, twice, then three times.

Statistically, more than 60% of adults in the United States report incidents of adverse childhood experiences (ACEs), including abuse, trauma, and neglect. Given our current population, we're talking about 200 million survivors.

I am one of them.

As Dr. Maté shared, "Stuff happens to us as children, negative things happen. Then, we adapt to those things by taking on certain defensive ways of being. And then, we live the rest of our lives from those defensive modes. So, we're not actually experiencing the present but constantly reliving the past from a perspective that we acquired when we were helpless and vulnerable children."

He pointed out that the more sensitive a child is, the more she will feel the pain or stress of her environment, the more she will be affected, and the more that will shape her experience. Even though I haven't accepted it for most of my life, I have always been "sensitive." What exactly does that mean? Well, as they smartly pointed out in this podcast, the word sensitive comes from the Latin word *sense* or *to feel*. Essentially, the sensitive person feels more.

I appreciated when Dr. Maté said that sensitivity also leads to more creativity. There's an upside! He also pointed out something else that hit really close to home. Sensitive people, especially those who have endured trauma, are far more likely to be high performers—successful on the outside while anxious, depressed, and frustrated on the inside. This pretty much summed me up to a T.

In a professional development program I was taking around the same time, one of the faculty had written a book on trauma sensitive mindfulness. There they were again, those words: trauma and sensitivity.

> *Sometimes we develop symptoms that extend past a traumatic event. This can include ongoing flashbacks...or volatile emotional reactions that emerge without warning. Some kind of alarm system doesn't switch off, and a traumatic experience comes to wreak havoc with our body and mind.*
>
> *This is known as posttraumatic stress—an experience where traumatic symptoms live on past the traumatic event. Because we are unable to integrate the experience, the imprint of the trauma follows us into the present, destined to replay itself over and over again. Posttraumatic stress fundamentally challenges the notion that time can heal all wounds.* (David A. Treleaven, *Trauma-Sensitive Mindfulness,* page 10)

Recognizing, for the first time in more than four decades, that I'd been experiencing posttraumatic stress helped me see two things: 1) it was real, and 2) I needed help. I couldn't work harder to fix it myself, like I'd done a million times before. Within a week, I hired a psychologist to help me recover.

RESEARCHING LIFE

I READ *The Official Preppy Handbook* early in the 1980s. No one told me it was meant to be ironic. Despite its origins in the humor section of the bookstore, I saw it as a how-to manual for living a good life. Boarding school, old money, summers in the Hamptons, families who arrived together on the Mayflower...belonging. If I followed the instructions, I, too, would belong.

I did what I could to blend in, to not be seen, while trying to reconcile the fact that I never, ever would. I was the girl whose dad died. When my mom started dating my future stepdad, I was the girl whose parents weren't married. I was the new girl, the girl who always cried, the girl who packed her own lunches—weird in first grade when I brought a blood sausage sandwich and everyone else had a PB & J or bologna and cheese on Wonder bread. I was the girl who had to start wearing a bra in fifth grade, the girl whose mom shopped at thrift stores, the girl who had 72 chickens in her backyard and sold eggs to her neighbors. If only I were more like everyone else, I wouldn't feel so bad.

I was doing all I could to fit in and get the "gold star," while deep down believing there was something terribly wrong with me.

TIPS FOR BEING POWERFUL AND SENSITIVE

IN MY LIFE, BEING SENSITIVE felt like something to overcome, rather than celebrate, something so much easier when kept hidden from others even though everybody must have known or assumed because I kept to myself and cried all the time. Bearing the pain of knowing and feeling how and what others feel and not knowing what to do about it, doesn't always feel like a party or a superpower.

It took many years, but I reached a point where I realized there was nothing wrong or weak about being sensitive. And not only was there nothing wrong with me, I was far more powerful than I had thought. Learning how to harness this became a practice.

Here's what I've learned:

(1) Food and nutrition matter as a sensitive person, especially when sick. Hunger is another stimulus that stresses my system

(2) The difference between someone who is sensitive and one who is not: we're all aware—empaths can

often identify which emotions are ours and which are not.

3. My body is always telling me things—am I listening?

4. When I know what works for me with food and exercise, it's okay to stop experimenting. I am not required to innovate.

5. Being aligned requires consistency and regularity. I feel better when I don't deviate from habits and routines that support my well-being.

6. I need support. We all do.

7. We all have within us the tendency to go back to old places and habits. I latch onto what I don't want because it's a habit.

8. Laugh. When I forget to laugh at myself and the absurdities of life, it can feel like too much. Stay lighthearted.

9. Be awake, aware, and open to whatever unfolds. Life isn't linear, and planning and strategy aren't necessarily the right tools to find alignment. I can release my tight grasp and gently allow what is happening *for* me.

10. Of all the places I may focus my love and attention, I must begin with loving and being compassionate toward myself.

(11) To be aligned and integrated is not for the faint of heart. When on my path, it is important to pay attention and be gentle with myself to go deep.

(12) I can be terrified when I don't know what to do next—or excited!

(13) Because I *can* doesn't mean I *should*. Shuck as many "shoulds" as possible.

(14) I can be in charge of my energetic experiences as much as I can of my physical or emotional ones. I don't need to feel like I'm at the mercy of my intuition, energy, or emotions.

(15) I can ask for help even when I don't know what I need or what questions to ask.

(16) Life is happening no matter what I feel or think about it.

(17) Clear out what's not working to make space for what's new. I can't be filled up when my cup is already full. I can't learn more until I first learn to become empty.

(18) The more I can let go of what's not mine, the happier and more at peace I am.

(19) There is only so much stress I can take on at once.

(20) Presence heals.

(21) Expectations limit my possibilities.

⑨22 Energy moves fast; bodies move slowly. Allow time to realign and integrate.

㉓ When I'm in balance, what needs to happen happens.

㉔ Having more awareness of sensitivity is *not* an invitation to be more precious about it.

㉕ The only thing wrong with me is that I *think* something is wrong with me.

WEIRD IS GOOD

Why fit in when you were born to stand out? – Dr. Seuss

I WAS IDENTIFIED AS GIFTED and placed in advanced classes beginning in sixth grade. I recall my mom disagreeing with my teachers and telling them—or at least telling me—that I wasn't that special.

I cried during the placement interview. I thought being gifted was something you had to work hard for and earn. It certainly didn't feel that way when I breezed through the school psychologist's questions and, at the time, didn't feel like I was getting any of the questions right. I didn't understand that my brain worked differently, even though none of the other kids in my regular class understood my jokes.

My life started changing for the better when my teachers took an interest in and began advocating for me. I slowly started to accept myself as the "special" person I am. Sixth grade was awesome.

(1) Everyone was a little bit weird; I wasn't the weirdest one.

(2) I felt understood.

(3) I belonged.

With the newfound confidence of being around other "weird" kids, I took a leap and ran for an elected office. Since I had managed my neighbor's campaign the year before, I had a taste of organizing people around a shared idea—I took charge of posters and campaign slogans and recruited a committee who believed that Michelle was the very best candidate for vice president. We were a committed group of grade school kids, and all eight of us voted for Michelle! (Unfortunately, no one else did. I had insider information since my mom was one of the parents counting the ballots confirming how Michelle lost her election bid, having only received eight votes.) Now, it was my chance to change the world in the most meaningful way I could—as school secretary!

Being the outsider I felt I was, and with an electoral loss in my recent history, I was obviously not assured the vote. Though I recall one of the most popular boys at our school whispering in my ear, his breath scented with Oreos from lunch, *I voted for you,* I lost the campus election, but my classmates, my new tribe of the slightly weird, instead chose me to represent them on the school's student council.

I never would have believed that, in the end, seen for who I was and being myself—the new girl with 72 chickens—I was more accepted, not less.

A LETTER FROM MY FUTURE SELF

DEAR 2008 KAREN,

Wow! What a big day today was for you! You registered a domain. Such a huge milestone to mark the beginning of your new career! Congratulations. It might not seem like it, but it's a really big deal. Right now, you don't know what you are going to say or what this space will become, but you believe in an idea, and you are putting yourself out there. Good for you!

This past year has been really hard for you, and not in the way you thought it would be. You always knew you'd go back to work when the kids were both in school, and now they are, and so you have.

You are caught up in feeling that you are not the same person as you were before you had kids, and you are struggling with your identity and how you relate to your work. I'm really sorry about that. I wish I could have been there for you to tell you that you are just as wonderful and talented now as you were when your career was your primary focus. Though you don't see that, the people around you do. And here's the hard truth: *you are definitely <u>not</u> the same person you were* *five and a half years ago when you worked full-time and didn't have children*—you really have changed, and you are amazing!

Mothering has softened your edges, you love more freely and deeply than you knew possible. There is strength, conviction, and compassion at your core, a knowing calmness. You know what matters. All that was difficult about this transition has carried you forward to a new place—a website with your name on it! You are here, and you are onto something. Let's see what happens next!

I don't want to spoil anything of what's coming, but this coach training that you're starting in a couple of weeks is going to rock your world. I am SO excited for you! Don't worry about what you need to do, just show up and be yourself.

Here's what I know about the future: it's already happening. Exactly what will happen? You have no idea! But you can trust me. Why? I am your Future.

Without getting caught up in the details, I need for you to listen carefully about how to deal with an uncertain future: even though you don't know what's next, make plans anyway. Do things.

Get clear on what you want, what's important to you, and take steps in that direction. You might fall off the path. You might head down one path and find yourself compelled to turn in an entirely different direction. You might stop along the path for a picnic or to smell the flowers. Go ahead and savor those moments; they are all yours to enjoy. You might pick a spot along your path and start digging deeper and deeper to figure out what is beneath and around you, to gain the perspective of looking at where you are from another place. Figure out the best companions for where you are on the path. Mix it up. Look for a guide or two or three or seven. Find your internal compass. Follow it. See what happens when you don't. Listen. Look around.

If I told you what it's like over here in the future, you wouldn't believe me even for a second. It's magnificent and so are you!

What I now know of the future is this: you cannot conceive of what it will be, so play with what's possible and how you want it to be. Creativity and imagination are your allies; knowing the specific details of how it will happen and what it will look like is overrated.

Lots of love,

Your Future Self

WORKING GIRL

THE 1980s WERE THE PERFECT TIME for an overachiever like me to grow up. I had the best research material and sources of inspiration to learn how to be successful. The Enjoli perfume commercials of the late 70s and early 80s reinforced the stereotype of what it meant to have it all, as the spokesmodel sang, "I can bring home the bacon, fry it up in a pan." Popular media featured a certain kind of woman in movies like *Working Girl* and *Baby Boom*. TV shows like *L.A. Law* had powerful female attorneys and even *The Cosby Show* had a mom who was a doctor. I could see myself in these women—high performers with big hair and shoulder pads like me! I was well on my way to having it all. I went to work.

I started babysitting when I was twelve and worked four years solidly until my regular clients had to start competing for my Saturday nights with the boy I was dating. The subscription to *Seventeen* magazine I paid for would arrive in my mailbox, and I would read it cover to cover. I'd examine the ads to understand teen life, reading the articles as if a scientific journal.

Babysitting gave me a time and place to plan out my future. One family I helped had older kids who weren't available to watch their littles. At their house, I studied old high school yearbooks. What was the path to success? Who was popular? Who looked happy? I narrowed it down to three factors: academic achievement, athletics, and student government. I was already a good student, already on the leadership path, and a decent tennis player. I could do this!

I decided to get straight A's the second semester of seventh grade after discovering that doing so, much like being a class representative, actually made you belong by standing out, so I did that until the end of high school. People apparently love you when you shine (and have 72 chickens!). I was a part of the Academic Decathlon team for about a week until faced with the realization that being an academic competitor, even though I was very competitive, would sidetrack my path to broader acceptance, so I promptly resigned.

The extra credit to being accepted and feeling secure in oneself was having a boyfriend—a steady Saturday night date and a constant companion—so I did that, too. When you study high school yearbooks as primary source material, it seems like the logical next step, the right thing to do. Busy checking all the boxes, I didn't leave myself much room to figure it out along the way.

I studied a lot. My GPA was a compulsion. I was going to get a 4.0+ NO MATTER WHAT. Even when that meant living on three hours of sleep to prepare for exams or falling asleep on the couch Friday nights watching *20/20* while my friends were out at parties. I had a plan. Nothing and no one would stop me.

I was always trying harder, always raising the bar for myself, rarely meeting it. At some point, it became an ingrained habit, the obsessive behaviors simply a part of my personality. I never saw my need to achieve as a wound that needed to heal. How could I? Instead of healing from the trauma of losing my Daddy, I internalized it. In essence, I'd become my own abuser. I used overachieving and striving as ways to protect myself from having to depend on others, while securing their adoration and praise.

Navigating life through the lens of *how I thought it was supposed to be* is a lot of pressure for a child (or at any age, for that matter). It's one thing to create and build and do things because it feels good and right to do so; it's another to maniacally force outcomes and feel like the world doesn't spin unless you're in charge of its rotations.

A LIST OF THINGS CAPTURED IN A MOMENT

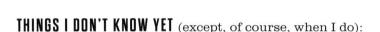

THINGS I DON'T KNOW YET (except, of course, when I do):

- anything about the future
- if I'm doing it right
- if I will run a half-marathon in September
- if I'll write a book
- how to keep talking when all I want to do is be quiet
- how to be quiet when all I want is to show how smart and capable I am

Things I am learning:

- how to listen beyond my five senses
- what slowing down looks like and how to stop trying to prove anything—to myself or anyone else

- how to feel all of my feelings and be with them

Things I am wishing for:

- patience

- action

- more color and beauty in my home and surroundings

- to fall in love with vegetables for my health and well-being

- more chances to roller skate and laugh out loud

Things that are getting on my nerves:

- getting in my own way

- being perpetually unconscious to things in my life and expecting different results

- being impatient about my own growth and process

- being impatient about my children's growth and process

- pettiness

Things that scare me:

- missing the big picture

- being so attached to the outcomes of failure or success that I don't pay attention to what really matters in the moment

- getting so lost in my ways that I don't get to do the work I was born to do

- taking it all too seriously

Things that are making me happy:

- the verge of summer

- my beautiful, amazing, glorious, precious children who are, as individuals and my babies, more than the sum of my dreams

- having a husband who uniquely raises the WOW! factor of my life in big and small ways every single day

- the freedom to create and explore my work and myself

- that the new local Whole Foods carries my favorite chocolate bar

- being filled with love

KAREN THE COLLEGE APPLICANT

Written in November 1988 for my college admission application. I was selected by UCLA to interview for their Alumni Scholarship. When I arrived and introduced myself, the volunteer greeter said, "Oh, you must be Long Coltish Legs."

KINDERGARTEN, 1976. My teacher kept us after class for being noisy, as six year olds sometimes are, and I cried. I had been quiet. I was afraid that my mother would forget me and I would be left at school forever if I did not get out of class on time. But there was really no reason for me to panic. The teacher had kept us after school so that she could present me with a Good Citizen award. That moment set a precedent that I would be destined to follow for the rest of my school days. From that day forward, I was known as Karen the Conscientious Student.

I did not realize that I was different, but the reputation of the Good Citizen followed me. I was a delight to have in class and worked well with other students throughout all of my primary education. What the teachers didn't see was the little girl who was afraid that she would make the wrong impression.

Once I passed through the trauma of junior high school by wearing the right clothes, knowing the "cool" people, and shopping at the "raddest" mall, I decided that I would try to be different, if not outstanding, in high school. I was caught in the excitement of having a senior boyfriend who was a runner. For no other reason, I joined the track team.

I knew, better than anything, that there were no official tryouts to be a member of the team. That was a vote in my favor. I hoped to be noticed as an incredible athlete. I forced myself to run because, after reading a variety of romance novels in between my favorite classics, I decided that I had "long, coltish legs." What I found was a body that would not comply with the rigors of athletic training and an injury that kept me from running for the next three seasons. I became team manager and statistician and felt that I was a true asset to the team. Since I would not be Karen the Athlete, I was satisfied as Karen the Organizer.

I spent many summers in tennis lessons wearing tiny skirts. I decided that since I loved to play the game, the best athletic team to join would be the League Champion Girls' Varsity Tennis Team. I lasted through the tryouts to make it, at least, on the Junior Varsity team. This would be my lucky break. But I played only occasionally when one of the starters was sick. As a junior, I was the number one player on the Frosh-Soph team. The tennis season did not allow me to prove my athletic prowess, but I kept the records straight and became assistant to the coach as Karen the Team Manager.

Although frustrated as an athlete, I found salvation in academics. Studying doesn't hurt. Studying English has been a challenge that I've especially enjoyed. For the last three years, I have taken advantage of my ability to write and to make sense. Until this year, my ideas have been praised and I have been complimented on my analyses. But I thought, after reading Conrad's *Heart of Darkness*, the hero, Marlow, saw the mysterious ivory trader Mr. Kurtz as a Christ-like figure, and my teacher told me that I was wrong. Perhaps I was. As of yet, I had seen English literature as gray, and now I have been told that it is, in fact, black and white. I intend to study English literature in college to better understand my own perceptions and to see different variations on common themes. I will probably hold my grudge until I can see the real answer. Until then, I will be Karen the Obstinate Student.

My pride and joy in school has been my position as Commissioner of Social Events in the Student Council Cabinet. Earning the title as a junior and retaining the position through my senior year was a goal that I set before even entering high school. My job is to present the Homecoming Halftime Celebration and Winter Formal. I do the job because I want to. It is against my nature to sit back and watch things happen when I know that I could do it all better. Even though much of my time is spent behind the scenes, I know I am respected for my commitment. After agonizing over finding a few gray hairs at seventeen, I threatened to become the Commissioner of Anti-Social Events, but both my Activities Director and I know that I do an amazing job. I shine when I am Karen the Leader.

And so I will go on, like a boat, as Fitzgerald said in *The Great Gatsby*, "...against the current, borne ceaselessly into the past." But I am no longer the pouty little girl that fussed over being a Good Citizen. I have grown to accept my distinctions as a conscientious student, an organizer, a manager, and a leader, but more than anything, I understand myself. I am Karen Cynthia Stevens, and I am ready to move on.

MAJORING IN LIFE

IN COLLEGE, I qualified for the honors program but decided to opt out. I didn't want to work that hard. I just couldn't do it anymore. I was so burned out after pushing so hard to excel in high school and preparing myself for life beyond. I figured *there's got to be a better way.* College could be a new beginning...a break from how I'd done it before. I no longer wanted to be the best academically. I didn't want the same type of relationship, which had grown tired and stale. For maybe the first time in my life, I found myself listening to my inner voice over expectations.

I started out as an English major, believing the writing would better prepare me for law school. Remember, I always had a plan. It looked a little something like this: graduate in four years, then work at a law firm to get experience, take the LSAT, go to one of the best schools in California, take the bar exam, pass it, be on track to be a lawyer and married at age twenty-five, have two kids (first a boy, then a girl) while on the partnership track, become a partner and maybe eventually a judge like my idol Sandra Day O'Connor, the first woman to be appointed to the Supreme Court when I was ten years old (and the reason I wanted to go to law school in the first place so I could follow in her footsteps). I'd be set for life. I would never have to worry about anyone taking care of me. I would work hard, and I would be okay.

What happened instead: realized that being an English major involves an oppressive amount of reading and writing, so I decided instead to major in being in a sorority, drinking, having sex, and finding the least demanding course of study most likely to help me land a job upon graduating. I changed my major to political science, not because it fascinated me but because most people going to law school majored in poli sci. I got sick the first quarter of my freshman year and had to reduce my course load while recovering. It would be fine, though, because I still had enough credits to keep me on track to graduate according to plan.

I feel like there were so many moments where my big plans should have come to a screeching halt, but instead I kept pushing through.

The minute I unpacked my bags at UCLA and Dykstra Hall became my address, I met a new guy. I was smitten…with Los Angeles, college, being on my own away from home, and this guy who looked at me with such an intensity I couldn't look away.

I was captivated by how different we were. I was a 4.0+ high school graduate on the honors track; he had transferred from community college. I grew up in an affluent suburb; his house was literally on what most people considered the wrong side of the tracks. We had incredible chemistry but, over time, developed a toxic relationship.

As I was preparing handmade gifts for him in celebration of our first year together, he was planning our first breakup. I didn't know how to *not* be with him—or how to not be with anyone—and I could not stay away. After the first breakup, he asked me to come back, and we were together again for nearly a year before he dumped me again. A few months after that, he won me back with big romantic gestures, and we stayed together through his graduation, then mine a year later. We broke up, got back together, and repeated the pattern as if doing so met the requirements for receiving my degree. Over the years, we fought loudly, publicly, and often. I once overheard someone describing us like "Ike and Tina."

Much like how Karen the Honors Student was an identity I was very attached to for most of my academic career, being Karen the Girlfriend was also the ultimate certification in belonging. Being half of a couple, albeit imperfect, supplemented the love I felt was missing while growing up.

FAILURE *IS* AN OPTION

What would you do if you knew you could not fail?

THIS QUOTE IS ATTRIBUTED to the Rev. Robert Schuller and has made the rounds of t-shirts, bumper stickers, and paperweights.

I've done a lot in my days never worrying about failure. Until the crash that ended my career, failure never seemed like an option I needed to consider. Then for a long time, failure was all I could think about when I thought about work. I could not imagine a world in which I could be successful as both a mother and a woman with a career, but here I am and it's okay—but there's got to be a better way than doing what I'm doing. Even though I've figured some things out, my heart isn't in it, and I bet I'm not the only one who has ever felt like this. I can't be.

The Reverend's words sit on my heart like a rock. I want to start a business to help mothers transition back to work, and I *do not want to fail*. I flip it over in my head. What would I do if I knew I could, and probably would, fail? What if the trying and failing and growing were more important than the achievement? What if taking the risk were enough, so long as the trial served up what I needed to know, and could fill my life with joy? What would I attempt if I could muster up every imaginable bit of courage, enjoying not only the prospect of success but also the novelty of doing something totally foreign and overwhelmingly exciting? What dream would I try to catch on a dare?

What would you do if you knew you could fail and you'd still be okay?

I've never started a business. I've always been employed, right until I wasn't. I have no idea what I'm doing, but I can't stop thinking about it, doing bits and pieces of research, and testing out the concept on my friends and family. I poured my heart out to a friend who believes in me so much that she's offered to help me make it come true.

There are days when I am filled with every confidence that not only should I be my own boss, I should become one of the *world's leading experts on mothers returning to work!* On others, I am overwhelmed with fear and doubt, which I then try to swallow or ignore, knowing full well that I won't get any farther ahead by doing nothing but worry. And I happen to excel at worry.

I realize that the biggest step in moving forward is taking *actual* steps. Sometimes the steps feel like leaps. And each time I take one of these leaps, I feel like I'm getting closer to the dream. The dream, the dare, it's out there, and it's mine.

There are skills I have, gifts innately mine, that make me who I am and would serve as the foundation of my new business.

I am a good listener. I am highly resourceful. I am really good at solving problems. I love helping people. I know what makes life meaningful. I am intuitive and insightful. I am able to help others recognize their own talents and roadblocks. I have reinvented myself more than once. I have revived my career after a significant leave of absence. I know how to organize people around a vision and a project. I give good advice.

Is this a business? I am inching toward it. I am really scared.

I am trying not to let perfectionism get in the way of my progress. Perfectionism is a hard habit to break, even after becoming a mother and exchanging it for dirty outfits, untimely tantrums, and embracing shit literally hitting the fan as the new normal, which is perfect because it's exactly how it is and there is no sense fighting with reality. I know that if I just decide exactly what it is I need to do, I would find a way to do it and be done, deciding that good enough really is good enough. But I am stuck in wanting to have every piece of it lined up "just so" before I feel I can confidently advance.

I am patient...or at the very least both patient and afraid. I wonder what will happen to my big little plan if I sit on it too long. Will I do something else, something more known and tangible to avoid the risk? Will someone else do it sooner? Better? When I consider *not* doing it, I shake it off. In every piece of me, I believe my idea is something worth doing and something both relevant and timely. I'm afraid if I don't do it, a world of opportunity would be missed. Fear again. Afraid of failing. Afraid of missing out. Afraid of staying the same. Afraid of what will happen to me if I don't follow my heart.

One day, I arrived at work, and while venting to a girlfriend about the dire straits of my life in that moment, I shared my new business idea and how I wanted to maybe become a leader in this field. She said, matter-of-factly, "You should do that."

Armed with my counseling degree, this wild idea, and the skills I could identify as uniquely mine, I truly believed I could help other people in my situation find a better way.

REALITY BITES

I GRADUATED IN FOUR YEARS as planned. I had taken the LSAT and secured my first job working in a law firm, where I anticipated I'd get a year of experience before going to law school. I had rented my first apartment and began work the day after receiving my diploma. (My tassel barely had time to settle after being flipped from right to left.) I was on my way.

Reality quickly changed my mind.

To my dismay (and the detriment of my becoming the next Supreme Court Sandy), I didn't achieve a high score on the LSAT, which limited my options. (Instead, the notorious Ruth Bader Ginsburg claimed my spot and became the second woman appointed to the highest court of the land after I graduated from UCLA. You're welcome, Ruth.) I hated working at the law firm and moved to another where I was even more miserable. I wasn't a fit for the work and detested the lifestyle and the grind of working for a litigator. I felt like the best of my days were over when I turned twenty-three. My car was broken into outside my apartment, and I didn't feel safe living alone anymore. So much for being the independent woman I imagined myself to be. "Ike" and I moved in together.

I was doing everything I thought was required to meet the standards of "successful," and I still wasn't happy.

At 4:31 a.m. on January 17, 1994 a magnitude 6.7 earthquake hit Los Angeles, taking out a section of the freeway, turning my hour-long commute into two. Did I need an actual earthquake to see how much I hated my life? Anything had to be better than this. Even doing *nothing* would be better.

Deviating from the plan a bit, I worked in temporary jobs for a few months, began to investigate graduate school programs, and looked for a way to be useful and actually help people. Working in law made me feel powerless.

What if I didn't follow my own plan anymore? Then what? How would I know how to move forward? I did what I do best—I researched. I hired a career counselor I found in the back of the 1994 edition of *What Color Is Your Parachute?* Over a few sessions, I discovered my values and what mattered to me in work and life.

Totally Delight in Using

Act as Liaison	Generate Ideas	Make Decisions
Analyze	Hostess	Mediate
Counsel	Implement	Plan, Organize
Deal with Feelings	Interview for Information	Perceive Intuitively
Evaluate	Make Arrangements	Prepare Food

Prefer Not to Use

Budget	Observe
Classify	Read for Information
Count	Transport
Expedite	Estimate
Monitor	

What else did I know? I liked volunteering on a local committee of UCLA alumni helping select future alumni scholars, and the most meaningful task I ever did working for the litigator was helping one of his pro-bono clients navigate through a landlord issue.

I arranged a visit to Loyola Marymount University. The school was small and local and offered a graduate counseling program through the School of Education. I had looked at psychology programs, but the best had a research focus, a field that, despite my skills, I had no interest in pursuing professionally. Plus, LMU offered rolling admissions. I wouldn't have to wait a year to apply—and another year in the agony of wondering, "Now what?"

INTUITION, TAKE THE WHEEL

IF YOU WERE TO GLIMPSE into the window of my twenty-three-year-old life, you'd see me pacing in front of the doorway marked "Graduate Admissions." It was a dark corridor of an old building. I walked back and forth down the hallway, past the door and not entering, easier to be lost in the shadows. I was so afraid to go in and say, "I don't know what I'm doing, but I think this might be right." Or that I might be rejected. Or that it might not be as easy as it seemed.

Two things that were really hard for me: 1) saying "I don't know," and 2) asking for help.

After pacing back and forth, in a sudden moment of knowing—a decision guided by intuition—my inner GPS instructed me to walk through the door.

Those steps stretched into a foundation of learning that is as much a part of me now as my eye color or fingerprint.

I met the LMU graduate admissions advisor and began the application process. As it turned out, he was a current student in the very same graduate counseling program I intended to join. We became friends, and he helped me navigate the system.

I told him about how I wanted to help college students figure out what they wanted to do next—because clearly I felt pretty lost when everything I thought I wanted to do was wrong. Wouldn't it be great to help others not make those same mistakes? He introduced me to a dean who had me begin a student retention project for the university, then another who had a position opening up in her department, where I was hired and then promoted within a few weeks.

Angels are everywhere.

BABY STEPS

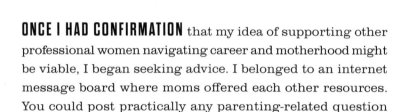

ONCE I HAD CONFIRMATION that my idea of supporting other professional women navigating career and motherhood might be viable, I began seeking advice. I belonged to an internet message board where moms offered each other resources. You could post practically any parenting-related question and start a conversation. I dug through the archives like an archaeologist, discovering a woman in Northern California who had a business helping mothers going back to work.

I believe that angels are real. The right person shows up exactly when you need them to help you through a situation no one else could. My business dream angel offered to get on a phone call with me and talk. In the early days of the internet before everyone and their kid had an online presence, it was unusual to meet a stranger and have her offer to sit and listen, expecting nothing in return.

As I took pages of notes, one thing she said stuck out: "Why don't you take one of those weekend coaching classes? I've heard Coaches Training Institute is good."

Coaching? Like sports but for people? I'd never heard of it. I had absolutely no intention of becoming a professional life coach. I had no idea the job even existed! But I knew I needed to do something better, I just didn't know what or how. I knew I wanted to help women like me, women who wanted career and motherhood to play nicely together in the same sandbox. I figured with my degree and experience—and a couple extra tools in my toolbox—I could start offering programs for women returning to work and launch my side gig.

So I checked it out. I was so nervous as I walked in the door for the introductory coach training. I went in feeling the familiar insecurities. *Who am I to start a business? I know nothing about starting a business. I am barely back to work, still struggling to figure out being a working mom. Could I really help people? Is this really a thing? Do people want what I want to give?*

Somewhere in the middle of the second day, the most amazing thing happened to me. We were doing an exercise around values (much like I did almost 15 years before with my career counselor), and the way my partner reflected what he saw in me back to me, acknowledging what was important to me, was a light bulb, aha moment. *Who I am is more important than what I do?! I have nothing to prove?!*

As I left the training room and drove home, the world had changed. My eyes were open wide. I saw possibility where before I'd seen nothing. I found my calling.

Looking back, had I a glimpse of how coaching would change me and everything else in my life for the better, I would have jumped through those doors! I started following the breadcrumbs of ideas (instead of having a plan), asking for help, trusting the connections I'd made, listening, and taking gentle next steps (instead of carving them into stone), and things got a lot easier. There I was, having no clue coaching like this even existed, and now it genuinely felt like it could be my life's work.

There was no way I could have known:

1. Building my own body of work is an extraordinarily powerful expression of who I am.

2. I would meet the most amazing people. I now have friends who are family, collaborators, and partners.

3. I would go through experiences that shook me to the depths of who I understood myself to be and come out stronger because I was masterfully coached and guided to know and accept myself with grace and compassion.

4. I would become aware of beliefs I didn't know I had—and find courage I didn't know I had to change the circumstances of my life.

5. No one's path is a straight line.

6. Being a powerful coach and leader is a place to *come from*, not a place to *get to*.

7. The business of coaching is as nuanced and as complex as the people we serve.

8. There are no "right" answers.

(9) There are no "wrong" answers.

(10) Learning happens in leaps and in flops.

(11) Listening is a highly prized skill.

(12) There is always another perspective.

(13) My Future Self is a wonderful teacher and guide.

(14) Metaphors are ripe and juicy access points to gain insights!

(15) Simply being in a room filled with dreams spoken out loud is empowering.

(16) Presence is priceless.

(17) It's not what you learn; it's how you integrate what you learn and live it that changes your life.

(18) The world is filled with infinite possibilities. Go forth and create!

(19) You are more than you will ever know.

(20) Do it now. It's time, and you are ready.

Over the course of this weekend, I learned how to listen and to hear. I was seen, not as the sum of my accomplishments, but instead by the light that shined within me as I spoke of what mattered most to me. Because I was seen, I could see others.

I took the CTI fundamentals course almost exactly six years after the fateful accident that changed the entire direction of my life and took a huge chunk of my identity with it. Then, I couldn't recognize myself. Now, I began to see myself clearly.

WORK 10, LIFE 3

LIFE WAS STARTING TO MAKE MORE SENSE.

In the fall of 1994, "Ike" and I went to Hawaii. We'd each saved $5 a day for a year and had enough to pay for a garden view condo and a discount flight to Maui. It wasn't like family vacations growing up, but we did it together.

We were playing at being grown-ups, doing things we thought adults were supposed to do. We had jobs, paid our rent on time, bought gifts for all our friends' weddings. We were fine, we'd settled into a new rhythm and no longer fought as frequently. He worked six days a week and golfed on Sundays. I went to school at night after work and studied all weekend. It felt like we were living separate lives.

In Maui, everyone, I mean EVERYONE, assumed we were newlyweds. We were not. Getting married would be the natural progression in our relationship, and it made me sad that while all our friends were getting married, we weren't. I hated being asked about it. I was embarrassed and ashamed that I hadn't yet achieved one of the greatest markers of success at this stage of life. *Why weren't we engaged yet?* I longed for that form of love and acceptance. I realized he wasn't ready to propose, and we disagreed fundamentally about marriage. Eventually, I wore him down, and we went and chose my engagement ring. Not romantic, but it worked. A few months later, in front of the fraternity house where he'd yelled at me, I'd slapped him, and we'd often held hands sitting atop empty beer kegs, he proposed. Of course, I said yes. Getting married was the next thing on my list.

As time passed and we grew closer to our wedding date, we began arguing more, disagreements often ending with one of us—usually him—storming out of our apartment and leaving for hours, sometimes days. While we should have been growing closer as we prepared to spend our lives together, we disagreed on almost as much as two people could. I pushed through the discomfort and kept on planning our magazine-perfect wedding.

In my Master's program group counseling class, I remember opening up about my upcoming wedding. *If I could, I'd do it differently. Maybe outside on a beach instead of the grand hotel affair, small and intimate, including only those who meant the most to us, not everyone on both sides of our families.* But this wasn't the plan or how I decided it had to be. I felt trapped in the life I'd created, but since I'd created it, and being as stubborn as I am, I felt I had no other option than to follow through.

While driving to work, I daydreamed what I would do if we finally broke up, whom I'd stay with, what I'd tell people—not the normal things you fantasize while preparing to walk down the aisle. Once I finished my Master's degree, I could go anywhere. I'd travel, see friends, move to the beach or maybe

Boston, if one of my friends got into Harvard for graduate school, because I could work at any university and Boston had so many.

After one epic fight, I remember telling my girlfriend, "I keep waiting for the other shoe to drop." A week later, it did.

It was the Saturday before Christmas, five months before we were to be married. We had a venue booked, bought the perfect bridal gown and bridesmaid dresses I'd found in *Modern Bride*, hired all our vendors, and were in the process of choosing from a pile of sample invitations and save-the-date cards. He walked in the door, looked at me, and said, "I think we should postpone the wedding."

My response: "I think we should call it off."

We had the most loving conversation of our relationship that night, of how neither of us truly felt like we could be ourselves around each other. We agreed how we would split our property, how he would take over our lease, and I would cover the lost deposits from the wedding. We wanted different things, and he never felt like he could be who I needed him to be no matter how hard he tried. He was right. I gave back the ring, packed my bags, and left for the last time. We spent six years together. Now, I was free.

I called my parents from a payphone at the grocery store around the corner from our apartment. "I'm coming home," I said. "It's over."

INTUITION LOOKS LIKE THIS TO ME

I SEE PICTURES IN MY MIND, sometimes a word or an image, even a scene from a movie will play in my head. Depending on whom I'm speaking with, if I feel it might be useful to share, I will. Sometimes I have a gut feeling or an unfamiliar sensation in my body, and I get a sense that there's information available from the feeling. This is how I would describe being intuitive if I tried. I don't usually try. It gets weird, fast.

I didn't know my way of receiving information was a "thing" until the day I did.

Intuition was taught in the curriculum of my coach certification program. Over the phone, our teacher instructed the class to listen to her tell a story, paying attention to any images, words, feelings, or sounds unconnected to the details of her story that occurred to us as she spoke.

Family drama was the subject of her story. As she told it, I could feel how broken and sudden the experience seemed to her. When she asked for feedback and what we noticed, I shared what I sensed in the subtext of the story: "It was like a glass shattered."

"That's exactly what happened," she said. Family argument at a wedding, someone threw a glass. After that, people stopped speaking to each other.

The story felt like the glass crushed at the end of a Jewish wedding. Something broken can never be unbroken.

PREPARING TO FALL IN LOVE AGAIN

WITH THE HOLIDAY SEASON UPON US, my childhood best friend, Lynnae, was home from graduate school when I called my parents to say I was coming home. Her family lived a few streets away from mine. Like I'd done a hundred times before, I dropped off my bags and went to her house to plan what was next. She was raw from a breakup, too.

Her parents fed us dinner, and we retreated to her room like we always did, only this time instead of playing with our hair and makeup, we made lists.

I never EVER wanted to make the same mistakes again. I had compromised on so many things that mattered to me, I had given myself away. *Who was I with him? Who was I alone? What had I missed?* I needed to write down what I wanted in a relationship so I wouldn't get caught up in chemistry and forget what was really important. When we were done, my list included more than 100 qualifications, written double-sided on three sheets of legal paper.

After I wrote the list, I swore off being in another relationship until I was ready, and since I had no idea how to evaluate that, I enlisted a group of girlfriends to keep me in check—the ones who I would have ignored had they dared to tell me how bad my last relationship was but now I was willing to listen to because they were right and I had been wrong. I'd spent three years with the high school boyfriend followed immediately by six years with "Ike". I was twenty-five years old and ready to take my life back, to take a leap, and this time, my plan wasn't entirely dependent on me and how I thought life was supposed to be.

THANK YOU, OPRAH.

WITHIN WEEKS of when I signed up for CTI's leadership program, the Oprah Winfrey show had taken its final bow after twenty-five years on network TV, and the Oprah Winfrey Network (OWN) was airing original programming. Among its early shows was my favorite *Finding Sarah*. Celebrated author and life coach Martha Beck took Sarah Ferguson, the Duchess of York, through a series of experiences to discover herself and rebuild her life—from dog sledding in the Yukon to exploring leadership while working with wild horses at a resort in Arizona.

Leadership development with horses!! While my new business was in a lull, I had been looking for a place to volunteer with horses. It had never occurred to me that you could do professional development with them. Certainly not something that fit neatly into a logical plan or how I thought it was supposed to be—and, yet, my intuition totally got it. The work was so profound, someone *had* to be doing it.

As a teen, I volunteered my summers at the Orange County Riding Center (now the Shea Center for Therapeutic Riding), which was then known as "a therapeutic horseback riding program for handicapped persons." In the company of equine therapists, a stable filled with gentle and patient horses, and children living with severe physical disabilities, I witnessed miracles. I watched kids who lived with limited movement among a myriad of restrictions become lighter and freer than anyone could have imagined when they were with their horse companions.

The work was not easy. The days were long, hot, and dirty. Unlike the fantasies of horsemanship I imagined while lazing on the couch reading *Black Beauty*, my work at the center involved mucking stalls, cleaning tack, and spending more time than I'd have thought possible stepping in manure—not your average suburban girl summer.

I loved it!

I remember a client at the center, a boy about my age who was confined to a wheelchair with cerebral palsy. He did not speak, at least not in a way my ears could hear. The preparations and maneuvering that took him from his mother's well-equipped van out to the trails were considerable. It was difficult for me to watch him, not having had any prior experience with someone so severely impacted by this disorder. It pained me to imagine his pain.

On a horse, he was a completely different kid. His smile was infectious. Warmed and transported by his steed, he relaxed and softened in musculature and demeanor. He radiated joy. He was free. The horse changed him. The memories were stored in the treasure chest of my heart, reminding me to believe in miracles. Those memories fueled me when I needed a miracle of my own.

I'M FREE

THINGS I DID AS A FREE WOMAN, loving life and this new identity at the ripe age of twenty-five—unmarried, feeling far from having a boy and a girl, and on a different career track that definitely wasn't going to land me a seat on the Supreme Court:

(1) Traveled: San Francisco, San Diego, New York, Palm Springs, Santa Barbara, Mexico, Puerto Rico. If you were going somewhere and wanted company, I was there. Let's make it a girls' trip!

(2) Moved: from the shared apartment to my parents' house to a friend's futon to a beach house I shared with roommates.

(3) Studied: I accelerated graduate school to finish as soon as possible, which meant I doubled up on classes while working full-time.

(4) Dated casually: I went out with all the people who were interesting to me and on my radar but in the past off limits because I was always in a relationship. I had the freedom to say yes and

no because I was not focused on being half of a couple. I broke a few hearts.

(5) Journaled: I examined my thoughts, wrote lists of songs I wanted to hear when I was in love again, glued in photos of things that made me happy.

(6) Got therapy: enough to notice that some of the patterns in the failed relationship mirrored unresolved issues with my mom.

(7) Bought rollerblades, saw every movie I wanted to see, read fiendishly, cooked, took on embroidery projects, cat sat, made new friends.

(8) Grieved and mourned the relationship, healed, moved on with my life.

Everyone I met and dated that year was measured up against The List. For a woman who had lost her way, it was a helpful grounding tool to stay true to myself and not ignore or overlook the red flags—like the one guy who had been cheated on by his last two girlfriends, the guy who wanted a serious commitment after our first kiss (not first date, first kiss), the guy with much better hair than mine, the one who asked me what I ate for breakfast to be sure it fit his regimen, the one who humbly bragged about his salary and dating history (*I'll never tell you my numbers*...um, I wasn't asking), the one who assumed all women from Southern California were shallow and uncultured, the one who played games and only called when he knew I wasn't around to answer, and the one who never called.

Before the guy and I called off the wedding, I was willing to overlook qualities or behaviors to stay in the relationship—until I couldn't. After the breakup, and writing my list, I took a break looking for forever. I'd already done that. I wanted to explore. I had a sense of humor about it. Dating was fun and funny and quite entertaining.

When I gave myself the permission to not be so serious, I was able to be honest about what was and wasn't okay for me.

DATING 101

I DECIDED TO TAKE at least a year off from being half of a couple and didn't want to end up committed again accidentally, habitually, or by default. It was like a gap year, but instead of postponing college, I was postponing a potential marriage. After a year, I felt ready to try again, and my wise council of girlfriends agreed.

I had an idea of how it was going to work differently this time. Here were my secret steps:

Step 1. I took care of my whole self—physically, emotionally, and spiritually. I felt amazing. I no longer felt like I needed someone else to make me whole.

Step 2. I was unattached. I signed an oath committed to finishing my Master's degree before I would be in another relationship, and I was one semester away from reaching the goal line.

Step 3. I was open. I had gone out with everyone I knew and all of my roommates' single friends. I decided I would have to meet someone through one of my new friends or work friends, assuming the single men in their lives would be pre-vetted and share common interests if we shared common friends.

Step 4. I closed open doors and burned bridges. It turned out one of the guys I dated had a very hot friend. I quickly ended potential entanglements with both in one swift move of giving the friend my number.

Step 5. I said yes. A girlfriend needed a +1 for a party? I'm in. Another was celebrating her engagement with a bunch of friends, and would I like to join? Absolutely.

I couldn't have known my secret recipe would work as quickly or as well as it did. My inner guidance was turning into a reliable co-pilot.

IT WAS A DARK AND STORMY NIGHT...

WINTER IN LOS ANGELES IS SPECIAL. One day, it's beach weather. The next, it could be pouring rain, flooding the streets, all the local news reporting *Storm Watch*.

January 25, 1997 was a rainy night, one where most would stay home. I was brave and already going out with Monica from work (see steps #3 and #5).

In Monica's group of friends, I was invisible. It was great going to cool places with a built-in crowd but terrible for dating. That Saturday night, we caravanned from a house party in West Hollywood to a one-act play in Hollywood to a swing club in Los Feliz for another party.

The Derby was one of those legendary Hollywood relics that had become relevant again during the resurgence of swing dancing, popularized by the 1996 indie movie *Swingers*. The place was notoriously cool, but I was not, especially among Monica's friends. We stood in an outrageously long line—a DMV-length, *Star Wars*-opening-night sort of line—bumping umbrellas outside.

I was bored and ignored. If I hadn't been Monica's designated driver, I would have called it a night and gone back to studying like I did every other Saturday night. Except I really didn't want to. I loved my outfit and really wanted to see inside the club. I'd never actually seen the inside of a club.

Monica left me to hold our place to see if she knew anyone at the front of the line. I glanced down the hill to my left and saw someone in a serious coat who was also checking out the line. As I gazed at serious coat guy, I said in my mind, "He's cute, I wonder if he's The One."

Within seconds, Monica was grabbing me to run to the front of the line, and at the same time, serious coat guy was trying to pay my cover charge because both he and Monica were on the guest list, and I was not. I looked at him, puzzled, declined his generous yet confusing offer, and paid my own cover. Inside, we all went our separate ways.

The club was vibrating. Zoot-suited guys and pin-up girls were dancing fast to the sounds of Big Bad Voodoo Daddy. Monica and I went to the bar to take it all in and meet up with the birthday girl whom I'd met once before (again, see steps #3 and #5).

As we stood in awe watching the scene, Monica noticed serious coat guy. "I think we went to high school together, but I feel weird asking."

"I know I don't know him, so I'll go ask."

I walked up to serious coat guy, inquiring, "Did you go to Pali High School?"

He did. Did I? No, but Monica did for a year, and wouldn't you know it, they were both there to celebrate the birthday girl!

With that began a conversation that now spans more than twenty years.

HORSE REFLECTIONS: A CONVERSATION BETWEEN RAFE AND KAREN

By 2015, our life looked nothing like it did before. We went from having zero businesses to two and having two dogs at home in Los Angeles to having a herd of dozens of horses at our second home in Santa Ynez, California. People kept asking us, "What are you doing and how did you do it and why?" So I interviewed my husband as we drove home from Santa Ynez one weekend where we talked about our "better way."

RAFE: I felt like all I did before was family and work, and then I would do that until the kids were done with college, you know, and then I'd reassess and figure out what I really was going to do. But then what happens if you die? I mean, I hate to say it, but it's true. If you are slogging through every day looking toward retirement and hoping you don't die before then, that's fucked up. I'm just going to say it. It doesn't mean you've got to live like you are going to die, but I mean, you know. It was horrible.

KAREN: Well, honestly, if you kept living like that…I'm not going to say it would have killed you, but I don't think we would have been so happy.

RAFE: No, it would have been terrible. But listen, I had no interests that were interesting. I played poker. I felt really boring. I'm like, *I'm a guy who has a family. I'm a guy who works for charities*. That's nice. But what else is there?

KAREN: I remember when you were working with that one horse…

RAFE: Yeah, Gringo, he was cool. He spent his life as a trail horse, head down, nose to tail, he had no idea that you could have fun. He was a grinder, and I felt very much similar to that. Just grinding out every day and doing what I needed to do, getting it done, not feeling like I had time for playing. I remember he was a very serious horse, so I would try to have fun with him, and he'd be like, "Who, me? I work."

KAREN: I just remember, too, how I was talking to someone else about this horse they work with who had been a working horse this whole time, and then he was adopted later in life and he got the light back in his eyes, and that's what I think happened for you. This experience brought the light back. I had to create programs so people could see it—and feel it—for themselves, just like you did.

THE ONE

SERIOUS COAT GUY'S NAME was Rafe Pery. Rafe (rhymes with "safe") grew up in Los Angeles before going east for college (thus the serious coat). He moved back home to follow his acting dream, applied to graduate school, and now worked in the nonprofit sector.

We had more in common than anyone I'd ever met. I described him to my friends as "not a fraternity guy, has done theatre, sings, dances, loves shopping, isn't gay, isn't into watching sports."

I'd only known him two weeks when I realized he was the great love of my life. Within three weeks, we were having conversations about marriage, children, and religion.

How did I know?

Until I met Rafe, I could always predict the end of a relationship at the beginning. While the high school beau was very sweet, I wanted more edge. The college ex was all edge, but we had to work to find anything in common. The guys I dated before and after all had their merits and their flaws. When I met Rafe (who, upon later review, met all but two of the criteria from The List), I found his merits extraordinary and his flaws endearing. I still do. I found him fascinating. I would call him simply to hear the sound of his voice. Smart, funny, romantic, hard-working, devoted to his family, raised among strong women, loved travel, and, most importantly, loved everything about me exactly as I was.

We made sense together. There was nothing left unsaid, no bridge we couldn't cross together. As we began to know each other, we began to know ourselves more. I could not imagine an end, and I was happy.

IT ALL HAPPENED SO FAST

THE NEXT FIVE YEARS were the most wonderful blur, a whirlwind of finishing grad school, moving up in our careers, getting married, buying our first home, adopting our first dog, and expecting our first child.

Rafe had always wanted a dog, but I held out, saying I didn't think it was right for us to have a big dog in a small apartment. One brisk November day, a couple of months after we'd bought our first home, we were out shopping. We decided to check out a pet store, and wouldn't you know it, they were hosting a pet adoption fair that day!

I was a bit ambivalent about getting a dog. We'd just bought a house. We were settling in, getting used to our space and life as homeowners. We both worked full-time and weren't home a whole lot. But because it was important to my husband and would be such a great anniversary gift, I kept an open mind. And then I saw Daisy.

We were greeted by the sounds (and smells!) of what seemed like hundreds of very excited four-legged friends. There were big dogs, small dogs, old dogs, and dogs with special needs, all who came sniffing in our direction when we walked past their freshly washed kennels. One dog stood apart from the rest. She didn't bark, jump, or sniff like the others, putting on a show to market herself. She used a more powerful and effective strategy—she just looked at us. Hopeful. Kind. Soulful. We both knew that we wouldn't—no, *couldn't*—leave her there another day.

We filled out the paperwork, made a donation to the wonderful shelter (who also generously offered to comp us a cat, but we declined), and took our girl home. Her first day with us, she didn't bark. The second day, she did. The third day, we both had to go back to work. I missed her terribly. I pined for her. I worried about how happy she would be in our home. I talked about her to anyone who would listen, and at the end of the day, I raced home to see her.

She's a special girl, our Daisy. She made us a family.

It occurred to me that if I felt this strongly about our dog, I was probably ready to become a mother. By the end of the week, Rafe and I decided that we would begin trying to conceive. By the end of the month (though we wouldn't know for a few more weeks), we had.

Six months later, I fell apart.

THE CRASH OF 2002

I THOUGHT I WAS DOING THE RIGHT THING bringing my freshly blended chocolate soy milk peanut butter banana smoothie into the car with me.

What I didn't know was the urgent flare of red brake lights, the sound of screeching tires, and a traffic collision would splatter these nutritious ingredients across the dashboard of my 2001 Ford Escape and, in a moment, change my life forever.

I was 31 years old and five months pregnant with Jake.

Along with the new house, new dog, and new baby on the way, I was also newly working at an incredibly demanding job. I was the youngest executive on the leadership team of a nonprofit organization that served adults with mental illness, many of whom were also homeless. The environment, the job, and the people were challenging. Some days were actually life-and-death. I was accessible 24/7, and I loved it. I was proud to carry my phone and pager, knowing I was on call for any emergency.

On Friday, April 26, 2002, I was drinking my breakfast while driving to a routine ob-gyn appointment. I had a hundred things to do after the visit. As I was starting to think of the next 101-150 projects on my list, I caused an accident. No one was seriously injured, but it killed my career, and I lost a huge chunk of my identity with it.

Here's the conversation I recall with my doctor after the tow trucks left and Rafe drove me to the hospital to make sure we—the baby and I—were both okay.

Doctor: What happened?

Me: Some idiot was turning left where there was no turn lane. I thought he was going straight. Why wouldn't he just wait and turn at the light?

Doctor: No, Karen, what happened?

Me: I was drinking a smoothie. I was thinking about work. I have a lot going on right now.

Doctor: You need to be thinking about your baby.

Me: But you said the baby is doing fine. I'm fine. Work really needs me.

Doctor: Your baby needs you more. Which is more important?

Me: (silent)

Doctor: You can't work anymore.

Me: (silent)

Doctor: You're distracted. You don't realize how much stress you're under and what this is like for your baby. You're lucky it wasn't worse, Karen. It's time for you to go on maternity leave. I'll give you a couple of days to let this sink in, and on Monday morning you'll come back to my office, and we'll take care of the paperwork.

Me: But...

Doctor: Give this some time. You'll be okay.

According to Dr. Elizabeth Kubler-Ross in *On Death and Dying*, the five stages of grief begin with denial followed by anger, bargaining, depression, and acceptance. I cycled through the stages simultaneously as soon as I had nowhere to go and nothing to do.

How could this possibly happen to me? I was taken out of the game, not by choice but by circumstance. I rear-ended someone. Big deal. I was sure I could focus better if I tried harder, and there's no way I'd let it happen again. How could I be paid to *not* work? How could I leave my team when there was still so much to do?

Underneath these nagging questions was an unfamiliar feeling: relief.

INSIDE OUTSIDE, UPSIDE DOWN

WE CAN LOOK AT PIECES of our lives as separate and distinct like when we dump puzzle pieces out of a box. We know all the pieces fit together somehow, and we spend a lot of time flipping them over and turning them around to see where they really go.

When I was single, I started to experience what it was like to feel okay not knowing where the pieces fit and no longer completely recognize myself. But given the world I had constructed for myself over the past five years—where I had more and more people counting on me, and more and more people living better lives because of what I helped create—when I couldn't work anymore, I didn't know who I was. At all.

I didn't recognize my puzzle anymore. I could only see a bunch of pieces mixed up. It didn't make sense. I didn't make sense. There was no teacher to grade me, no end goal or milestone to tell me I had done my job well. I was a mother now. Just a mom. I did *not* have it all.

Nothing could have prepared me for what it would be like no matter how much I read or researched. I was stepping into a job I had zero qualifications for—and didn't 100% love the title. I knew being a stay-at-home mom was really important, but I didn't know how to mesh who I had always been with who I needed to be.

I had to put the pieces together without a picture to guide the process.

Over the next six years, I deconstructed and rebuilt myself. I didn't know I was doing it at the time, but I started paying attention to how I actually felt about my life, not just what was next on my to-do list. Not having a goal was humbling.

Oprah Winfrey was the girlfriend I sat with on the couch at 3:00 every afternoon while my baby was napping. I paused the show during one episode to ask myself the most important question I could: *Who am I?*

I fell into dark days of doubt while I was on my forced leave of absence from work. I knew myself by my ability to achieve. I expected I'd be gone a few months, but the break lasted more than five years.

The break broke me open.

Unable to do what I'd always done before (work, succeed, achieve), I was forced to take apart the puzzle of the person I thought I was to discover that I was so much more than each individual piece.

I had been used to measuring success in promotions and pay raises. After the break, I traded those metrics for the experience of living—actually feeling alive—in the day-to-day, even when I had no idea what I was doing or where I was going. I grew richer in relationships, self-awareness, joy, and a deeply grounded sense of purpose.

Forbidden to play my accustomed role, having nothing familiar left to define me and no boss to review me, I had to evaluate myself: *What did I love? What did I need? Where did I thrive?*

I had to listen: to the people around me who loved me, to my children who were not at all impressed by my résumé, and to a quiet, still voice inside me. I began to remember myself.

EXCELLENT ADVENTURES: A CONVERSATION BETWEEN RAFE AND KAREN

RAFE: That's what people need and that's what I needed to know—the horse experience reminded me I could still have some fun and do things that were a little bit crazy and feel good about it. Surfing was that for you. Who thought you were going to get people to surf for leadership development? I went, and I was terrible, but I played in the waves, and I had a great time. I got pummeled, but it felt great to just be pummeled by the waves.

KAREN: Just to be alive.

RAFE: Yeah, and just to do something different and not something run-of-the-mill. And just to give a plug for horses, I think every person should experience that—whether they are comfortable with them or not—if they want to learn about themselves really quickly.

KAREN: Of course, I completely agree, which is why I love my work. What I get to do with people is whittle things down and reflect things back. I can hear it in their voice when they are talking about something they love or talking about something they hate or talking about something they don't care about. I listen to the energy underneath what they are telling me. One of the best aspects of coaching is asking a question, letting people talk out loud, and asking, "Is that what you think? Is that what you mean?" or to be able to challenge them. One of my clients was telling me something that she was going to do that was going to make her happy, and I was like, "Hold on a second because you just told me x, y, and z about you, and now you are telling me that this is going to make you happy? That doesn't make sense to me. Explain to me how this makes sense to you." It's a lot of reflection and introspection. I think great coaches are going to help you find out who you are by doing things differently. I always say nobody hired a coach to stay the same. By the time someone hires a coach, they are often miserable about something. And miserable usually means, "My life isn't happy the way I want happy to be, even though I don't know what happy is."

RAFE: There is a tendency to associate money with happiness.

KAREN: It's not true.

RAFE: No, it's not true. And if you can figure out what you need to be happy and what you want to be happy, those things may be very different than what you currently have. I also wonder, and that's another question for you, what about for people who can't afford coaching? What do you do to find life's satisfaction? What would you recommend?

KAREN: You know, coaching is a great modality. Therapy is a great modality. If people can't afford coaching, sometimes their insurance will pay for therapy and very often therapy will help you find some answers. Don't discount therapy, even though I know there is still stigma associated with it for a lot of people.

RAFE: That's why I think everyone should get on a horse. And we don't call it therapy; we call it cowboys.

ALL ABOUT MY MOTHER

IF YOU ASKED ME TO DESCRIBE my mom at this point in my life, I would tell you she is creative, artistic, an amazing gardener, an involved and curious cook, a student, a traveler, and a good friend. She is also a terrific Nana! She is open-minded, open-hearted, and gracious, even when she thinks she is not.

Growing up, I focused on a lot of what she was not. I don't know that I knew her or that she knew me. I don't know that any child can ever truly know their parents while they're being raised. Our relationship will always be complicated because of the women we are and the traumas we have survived together and alone. We do our best.

A few short stories from our early years tell you about the mom who inspired me.

(1) It was the summer of 1983 when braces were installed on my teeth. The next day my mom took me to see a matinée performance of *Woman of the Year* at the Ahmanson Theatre in Los Angeles starring Lauren Bacall who had won the Tony for her performance of the role on Broadway. We sat in the orchestra section, and she even bought me

the soundtrack that we would later listen to all the time in her car. I felt like a grown-up and a lady. I'd only learn years later how much my mom hates musical theatre.

(2) We took another trip to downtown Los Angeles, this time to the jewelry mart, the day after my high school boyfriend moved out of state for college. I remember our quick trip to the ATM, leaving practically as soon as the sun came up so as to avoid the traffic, and the pearl studs I bought for $40. We didn't talk about how I'd miss him, how I'd manage without him, how he might be my first love but not my last, or what it meant to be so serious about a boy at such a tender young age. All we did was walk and shop.

(3) I'll never forget the moment I saw my proud mom jumping and waving her arms in the sea of thousands of parents in Pauley Pavilion at UCLA's College of Letters and Sciences commencement ceremony. From a distance, I could see her smiling through tears of joy.

Everything I needed to know, I learned from my mom. She showed me the wisdom and value of not buying retail ("Why would you buy this here when you can find the exact thing somewhere else for a fraction of the cost?"). For every special occasion, I had a new dress—but those were never bought off the discount racks. She taught me not only the basics of cooking but also the love of good food and, through our backyard farm, the difference between what you make yourself and what is store-bought. My mom is a master gardener (with an actual certification!). I did not inherit her green thumb, but I can correctly identify many species and varieties of plants from our nightly summertime walks in her garden, and I am passionate about seasonal produce as a result of her tutelage.

She has let me make my own mistakes and encouraged my worthwhile pursuits. Though my mom wouldn't have joined National Charity League on her own, we shared a commitment to making a difference in our community—she spent her hours improving the organization of the thrift store while I was a stablehand at the therapeutic riding center. Together, we delivered Meals on Wheels.

As much as I've learned from her, I'm also proud of the things she has learned from me, like when we were both taking pre-calculus and tutoring, and she told her students what I'd told her when solving problems—use the whole page! I still have the note she left for me on the day I lost the election for student body president (praising my courage for running against the most popular girl in school), a card she sent me my freshman year at college (reminding me to always be myself), and an email she sent when I was working at a facility helping homeless and mentally ill adults (amazed at my ability to keep a clear head).

I learned how much it meant to her to be a grandmother the moment she insisted on being at the hospital for the birth of my first child, even though I had stubbornly insisted I wanted no one there. She and my stepdad spent years driving thousands of miles to visit my children with the purpose of giving me time to myself, always bringing snacks and treats, games and adventures that have my babies rushing to see what's in Nana's bag.

We're probably more different than we are alike, but I wouldn't have picked anyone else to be my mother even if I could.

I INVENTED MOTHERHOOD

I CAN'T PINPOINT THE EXACT MOMENT when I became a mother, but I think I truly became a mom when Jake was eight weeks old.

Of course, I was more careful about what I ate from the minute I saw two lines on the pregnancy test, but that didn't make me a parent. Leaving the hospital with Jake strapped securely in his car seat didn't cement the bond either. Motherhood isn't a four-year degree; it is a process and has required continuing education from the moment Jake let out his first scream.

For more than nine months, I read books and articles and poured over the Babycenter message boards. I wore tailored maternity clothes, bought baby supplies, and prepared his nursery. I had an expertly packed, mommy-approved, overstuffed diaper bag ready before his due date. Then, he arrived, and I was stumped. Daddy would go to work, and I was home with The Baby. What was he old enough to do? What was I supposed to do with his floppy neck? Could he ride in a jogging stroller? What would I do with all this free time? What next? What now?

I had NO IDEA.

There is a point at which the books stop being useful and paying attention to this new person you're with gives you experience and you become the guide. I knew pretty well after our first outing what I needed in the diaper bag (extra diapers and wipes, a snack, maybe a change of clothes for one or both of us), and what I did not (everything else).

One day, Jake and I were sitting in a circle of women at a mom's support group at a local high school. Jake would not stop fussing. I felt anxious in front of all these "expert moms" and wondering what they'd think of me—The New Mom. Jake refused to eat, wouldn't burp, and couldn't be comforted by my gentle (albeit nervous) rocking. I became terribly self-conscious. No one else's baby made a peep, and I couldn't even do the basic mothering required to calm my own child. What kind of mother was I?! Embarrassed and frustrated, I stopped and looked down at Jake.

Looking up at me were the sweetest eyes and smiling face. I was his forever.

When our eyes met, something in me shifted. Obviously, I was always Jake's mother, but now I'd become his mommy—for probably the first time ever, I understood unconditional love. I just didn't know what to *do* with it.

People tell you that becoming a mom is this amazing, transforming experience, but it doesn't really hit you what exactly this means until you are home alone with your baby.

You think, "Okay, I've got the nursery set up, the sheets are washed, and that is where the baby will sleep." You don't imagine that the baby won't understand the differences between "night" and "day," or that she will need to sleep tightly cocooned and swaddled nestled close to your body for her first three months, especially after you swore you would never co-sleep. You can't conceive of how you will function on little sleep, no sleep, or sleep interrupted for several months, and sleep is only the beginning.

I remember feeling very lost, having not yet earned the title "mom," wishing I already had the answers. I thought it might have been better/safer/wiser if parenting were handed to me like Jake was after my C-section.

I eventually realized that some days are hard because they're hard, not because I'm a bad mom. Some days are easy and good, and that doesn't mean I'm the best mom on the planet either. I've simply learned how to parent my own kids, and we're all still a work in progress.

In my professional life before motherhood, I was confident and secure and made decisions left and right, but in my new profession as a stay-at-home mom, I barely felt competent. Beyond just being exhausted, I was isolated, lonely, and questioning many of the decisions I was making because I had never done anything like this before and feared that I was doing it all wrong.

Ideally, I'd have been handed my "official mom" certificate as I lay in the hospital bed looking at this new child of mine. Instead, it felt like I had to invent motherhood.

MOTHERHOOD REINVENTED

I USED TO SPEAK OF 2002-2007 as the lost years. I went from having a career that felt significant and important to becoming a stay-at-home mother with two brand new bosses who were extremely immature and incredibly demanding. While I don't know if I was depressed during this time, I do remember the strange relief of not having a "real job" after having pushed so hard to keep work the central focus of my life. Despite my lack of knowledge or preparation, despite the loneliness and confusion, I was surprisingly content.

Being a mother changed me. A part of me that was lost was found in unconditional love for my babies. Until I became a mom, I did a lot of things I didn't know how to do but always knew I'd figure out, either because I wanted to or because I had to. My life moved forward in what felt like a pretty straight line of being excellent at whatever was my goal, from school to work to career to marriage. How much could I take on before I could hold nothing else?

Now, I held Jake.

Jake was my constant companion, my tiny suit of armor. I surrendered to his impromptu naps on my chest, recognizing that the moments where he and I would be so close might not last forever. If it meant I'd lie on the couch for two hours while he slept on top of me and that was what needed to happen, it did.

I made up songs to sing to him when he woke in the mornings because I couldn't remember all the lyrics of "Mockingbird." Plus, he preferred "Blackbird" and The Beatles. It didn't matter. We were in love.

I remember the early months of his life not knowing what I was "supposed" to do and, for the first time, not really caring. I called the angel of a nurse at our pediatrician's office one day in a panic. "He's not doing what the books say he is supposed to at this age." Her reply: "I guess the books don't know Jake."

Being Jake and Ellie's mom disrupted all my patterns. The babies were neither impressed nor influenced by my proven track record of success. Me being myself, perfectly imperfect, was all they ever needed or wanted. No one was more surprised than I was that it took the act of creating two phenomenal humans to discover the one I always was.

THE RIGHT WAY TO PARENT

IN THE TIME THAT LAPSED between being childless, pregnant, a new mom, and then a mother of two, I gained some perspective. I was aware that I hadn't invented motherhood (at least not for all of humanity), though I still managed to harbor strong feelings about the "right" way to parent.

It took me a few laps around the block (and a few of the moms in my playgroup giggling at my well-stocked diaper bag) to learn that I didn't need to carry a digital thermometer, infant Tylenol, Benadryl, two changes of clothes (one for each of us), six diapers, a burp cloth, a bottle filled with water to mix exactly four servings of formula, a handheld electric formula mixer, three pacifiers, a fully-stocked box of wipes, five favorite toys, a bib, a placemat, and a 4 x 6 foot blanket every time I left the house. (This is not an exaggeration. It was a big bag. Very full and very much packed by the books.)

As an expectant parent, I watched an acquaintance of mine holding her newborn daughter while she slept and thought: *She should be sleeping in a bed. How will she learn to sleep on her own if her mother is constantly holding her?* I couldn't get over how widely my beliefs differed from her approach (and how sure I was of myself). How could we both be right?

Then, Jake arrived. He exceeded the standards. He ate well, slept well, grew consistent with the growth charts. Even though he was practically a "textbook" baby, I had his clothes neatly sorted by size—3 to 6 months, 6 to 9 months—and held off on putting him in them until he was the "right age." For some reason, I continued to be confused when the textbook didn't have a chart to help me see that my baby is my baby, and he is the size he is when he is that size (not when the labels say he is "supposed to be"). Slowly, I would learn to start raising my child (and reconstructing myself) off-book—as if preparing myself for the next big scene.

Enter Ellie. Ellie was not at all textbook. Within two weeks of her arrival, we began our semester-long education on colic. For seventeen weeks and four days, she only slept when swaddled and worn in a sling.

When the midwife remarked on my baby's absence at my (our?) six-week postpartum checkup, a time when most new moms can't wait to show off their sweet sleeping cherubs, I explained that I needed the break from her. I burst into tears, telling her of the screaming, the endless nights, her inability to be consoled, and how I simply didn't know what else to do. She looked at me with kindness and understanding and said, "It's hard to bond with a colicky baby." (An understatement to say the very least.)

I reasoned that my strong young independent Ellie didn't believe she was ready to be born, and since she didn't choose it, maybe it wasn't time. She didn't know how to soothe herself, but being close to me—to my heart and the sounds of my body—seemed to be enough. It had to be. It was all I had left. All I could give her was my heart.

I can only imagine what the other parents thought when they heard the details of our nightly ritual: wrapping her in a Velcro-fastened blanket, nestling her in a sling, holding her pacifier in her mouth while walking on a treadmill for as long as it took for her to fall asleep. I certainly remember what I thought a few years prior. Now, it didn't much matter what they thought, not that they dared to offer, because it's what worked for us.

This situation pushed me to my limits. More than ever before, I had to go within and trust myself. We were forced to invent our own ways to help our baby girl that, again, we couldn't have learned from any book.

Can there be many correct ways to parent? Of course. How else would we figure out what might work—or not work—if we didn't get to see it firsthand and decide for ourselves? Experience has proven to be a great teacher, better than some mothers I've met and almost all of the books I read. This parenting adventure offered me the confidence I very much needed—without the need to get it "right."

BEGIN AGAIN

AFTER GOING BACK TO WORK, hating it, and realizing there had to be a better way (even though I had no idea what I was doing or what to call it), I moved very quickly to accelerate my coaching business. With limited experience, raw talent, and an urgency to help end my own suffering and, hopefully, for people whom I could help, I went from not knowing anything about coaching to actually being useful.

My instinct was spot-on, but the practicalities were lacking. In hindsight, it took roughly four years to start a business, gain the technical skills to serve said business, learn how to effectively work with clients, and expand the business. It isn't a lot of time, and it felt like an eternity.

In 2008, while I was still employed, I founded Motherhood. Reinvented: *Who do you want to be when your kids grow up*?™. After finding my voice in my blogs and receiving so much resonance around what I was sharing, I felt I spoke for something bigger than myself or my family. I wasn't the only person struggling to reconcile identity, motherhood, and career—and I could help. I made beautiful business cards, paid more than I felt I could afford to launch a website, led workshops, and was featured in magazines and newspapers as the expert I thought I wanted to be on mothers returning to work. I was still in the grind of it and still unhappy.

Not only that, the women I thought I wanted to work with didn't want to work with me. I thought other moms wanted to go back to work like I did and would want help. They didn't. Personal development and professional growth were not in the budget, unlike highlights and Pilates. Things were not going as planned. The more I tried to work with moms, the less I wanted to. The more I worked with people who wanted to do something new and different, who saw obstacles and opportunities and their own ability to make a change, the more I felt like I was doing the work I was supposed to do.

When we met late in 2009, Carrie was an established coach living the dream. She was—and is—a badass entrepreneur, ambitious mom of four, working on her own terms, balancing career and motherhood, and making it look awesome. She was doing it differently—and living my dream. Her reputation preceded her so much so that, when I ran into her in a hallway outside the classroom where I was about to take one of my last coaching courses, I blurted out, "You're Carrie Kish!"

Carrie was a role model, a beacon of hope, and a shining example of what was possible for us newbies. I needed more of her in my life. Light reflects light. Carrie believed in me in such a generous and powerful way I immediately saw myself differently. She didn't see the obstacles I saw for myself. She saw me as the badass visionary I am.

Carrie was another angel, showing up exactly at the right time to help guide me through a situation I could never have imagined navigating on my own. She gave me opportunities I didn't know I wanted or needed. Because of her, I took chances I didn't know I could, which opened doorways I didn't even know were there. Carrie was like butter in a frying pan—she made things easier and better in ways I couldn't always see and thoroughly enjoyed.

In June of 2011, I got an email from the Coaches Training Institute. They were piloting a one-week leadership retreat as an introduction to their year-long program I very much wanted to attend and very much could not afford. The investment was much bigger than I could stomach, and Rafe's business wasn't stable enough to predict when or if we could. But a week? We could afford a week.

Carrie had done the leadership program years before, and since she stood as this lighthouse of possibility for me, when the email came, it was an easy yes. One great Carrie-ism: do the work in front of you. Another: you're exactly where you are supposed to be. And she was right, as usual. This retreat eventually served as the catalyst to completely deconstruct my first attempt of starting my own business and make space for what was about to emerge.

SWEET LITTLE GIRL

I CAN'T GET IT "RIGHT" with my daughter. Good thing I've learned that "right" doesn't matter anymore.

Moved into her Big Girl Bed, soon after her third birthday, Ellie is up, SCREAMING, once, twice, sometimes three times a night. She needs to pee. She's fallen out of bed. Now she can't find her bed. She's had a bad dream. She can't find her blanket. She's lost a sock. She asks if it's morning whether it's 8:30 p.m. or 3:30 a.m.

I do what I can. I find what is missing. I tuck her in tightly. I try to give her every security that she must feel she has lost.

Some nights, Ellie asks for me to hold her. I spend a few minutes in either her bed or mine, and we lay chest to chest. She has again found a way to be close to my heart. She still needs this from me, and though I'd never ask, sometimes I need it, too.

Had I known how quickly it would pass, maybe I wouldn't have rushed through her babyhood wishing her older and less dependent. How I'd miss the routines that gave us the smallest shards of sanity during her colic. How I'd long for the feeling of lifting her growing body, then placing her down gently in her crib at the end of each day. Those days are long gone.

In a cabinet far out of reach, I kept a supply of her pacifiers moved out of sight when her pediatrician told me it was time for her to give up her "night night," not expecting that she'd use them again but stunned that she never asked. One day, she won't ask for me either.

Today she does, and it is that which I cherish.

My heart is full.

ACCOMPLISHMENT JUNKIE

I WAS LOOKING AT PHOTOS and two thorns kept poking at me. First, was I always so blue? And second, what happened to my big plans for the future, the ones that don't revolve around my children?

As I put the pictures back into their sorority-girl puffy fabric-covered padded albums, I noticed something else. Evidence shows that I have been happy, not always critical and brooding. And one thing in common in my shining moments: a sense of accomplishment!

Each of these moments comes with its own fanfare, a sense of achievement, satisfaction, and success. Looking at my face, I may well have been saying: "I can't wait to tell the world about what I'm doing and how freaking great this is!"

As a person who loves a good checklist, I know that I am motivated by accomplishment. I am a high achiever. I like being an expert and a resource. I like mastering new skills. I like a clear path. I obey rules, and instructions are my guide. I like a beginning, middle, and end.

I don't improvise in the kitchen. I follow recipes knowing that if I do the steps in order, I will get the desired results. I am a process person. I like results. I like believing I can determine my own outcomes. I do not like uncertainty or taking risks. I like to know that if I'm going to try something, I will succeed. A favorite movie? *The Sure Thing.*

Beginning. Middle. End.

Motherhood is not this way.

In the quiet moments, I am "just a mom." No pressure to perform, and all the time in the world to discover the depths of the rabbit hole I'd fallen down for most of my life. The one paved with the idea that my worth was determined by the sum of my accomplishments, my existence a product of how much I could do and how worthy I could prove myself to be. I'd worked my whole life to compete and complete things that made me feel like I mattered. *Who am I without something to overcome? Something to master?* I hate to say it, but there's no "overcoming" or "mastering" motherhood.

When we don't know who we are, we tend to fall asleep at the wheel of life. We either act as if what we do and who we are doesn't matter at all or that it's the only thing that matters. We search and seek outside ourselves to find an answer that lies within.

I love my children, and I love being their mother, but a lot of this stay-at-home parenting gig is a grind. In the five years since I left my outside employment, I've not had one single raise or bonus. I've not had a report card with all A's nor been listed on the honor roll. I didn't even get into *Who's Who* of outstanding mothers in America. Motherhood is not a competition, but I can see why some try to make it into one. We want to be valued and esteemed. We want to be lauded and congratulated on raising wonderful children and for taking the time to give it our best efforts, whatever those efforts might be.

Motherhood is as filled with uncertainty as it is with dirty diapers and tears. Every day is a gamble. Will he have a good day or bad? Will she be the terror of Mommy & Me again? Will they nap? If they do, will they go to bed? If they don't, will they have nightmares? Will they eat? Are they growing? Will someone get hurt? How will I get through?

Beginning. Middle. End?

I keep hoping that someone else has the answer that I've missed or overlooked, but I keep coming back to the same realization.

It's me.

No one else gets to figure out how to be a mother to my children.

And no one else is supposed to figure out how to make me happy.

This is the life I always wanted.

Education.

Marriage.

Children.

Now that I'm here, I have to figure out what I want next.

When I dreamed of these babies, decorating their nurseries in my mind, it never once occurred to me what it would take to preserve myself, to be a woman with children, and not just a mother.

MORE THAN "JUST A MOM"

I'VE WRITTEN A LIST of what I love because sometimes I forget that I'm not "just a mom."

100 Things I Love (in no particular order):

1. cupcakes
2. magazines
3. monogrammed accessories
4. lemon bars
5. sourdough bread, warm, with butter
6. sorbet
7. goat cheese
8. great meals
9. Lost Coast Great White Ale
10. tasting menus
11. going to the movies

12. *Grey's Anatomy*
13. aseptic packaging
14. buying clothes for my kids
15. shoes
16. feeling strong and lean
17. the good kind of soreness after a workout
18. my hair color
19. pajamas
20. the sweet, fresh, wet smells of a clothes dryer mid-cycle, rain, lavender, and my children's hair after a bath
21. bubbles
22. Paris
23. French Provençal table linens
24. that I met and married the man who considers it his primary objective to make me happy
25. Hawaii
26. travel
27. skiing
28. new snow clinging to the branches of every tree, blanketing the landscape in shades of white and gray

(29) tennis

(30) pedicures

(31) tomatoes

(32) crossing items off a to-do list

(33) reading

(34) winning at poker

(35) a perfectly chilled glass of chardonnay on a hot summer day

(36) champagne

(37) long walks and talks with girlfriends

(38) feeling seen, known, and understood

(39) key lime pie

(40) looking at my baby pictures

(41) the story of how Rafe and I met

(42) our wedding album

(43) Buffalo wings with bleu cheese dressing

(44) surprise packages and letters

(45) irises, tulips, and freesia

(46) watching the sunset anywhere near the Pacific Ocean

(47) listening to Hawaiian slack key guitar music

48. caramel apples
49. Disneyland
50. onion dip and Ruffles potato chips
51. TiVo
52. Oprah
53. cuddling with my boy, watching movies and reading together
54. Santa Barbara, especially its zoo and La Super Rica
55. afternoon tea
56. taking cooking classes
57. Surfas cooking supply store
58. Impressionist art
59. Coca-Cola Light
60. room service
61. everything my baby girl utters, from her silly songs to her unique toddler-ese phrases
62. holding hands
63. pearls
64. diamonds
65. a little black dress

66. pale green, periwinkle, indigo, rose
67. Tchaikovsky and Mozart
68. Debussy's "Clair de Lune"
69. soundtracks
70. sushi
71. cookbooks
72. worn-in jeans
73. lipstick
74. when my children are laughing and playing together
75. Target
76. Trader Joe's
77. internet food blogs
78. Daisy
79. that my children are developing loving, trusting, and independent relationships with their grandparents
80. *Sesame Street*
81. the library
82. my Volvo
83. UCLA

- 84. chips and salsa
- 85. margaritas with salt
- 86. cashmere sweaters
- 87. New Year's day traditions including the Pasadena Tournament of Roses parade
- 88. Kidspace Museum
- 89. bags and purses with lots of compartments
- 90. the view from our office window
- 91. Thanksgiving dinner cooked by my mom
- 92. my comfy chair
- 93. blue ballpoint pens
- 94. popsicles
- 95. making sandcastles in the sand
- 96. my kitchen
- 97. freshly cleaned carpet at home
- 98. soup
- 99. San Francisco
- 100. steak

THE UNSUNG HERO

WHILE I WAS STRUGGLING to figure out who I wanted to be in my evolving business, what I was supposed to do, whom I was going to work with, how would I ever earn an income, why was I still not happy, Rafe was also building his consulting business. The work was flowing. He was busy, but he wasn't happy either. Our lives were short on magic, and the love of my life was bearing the burden. I could see it and had absolutely no idea what to do.

I remember a conversation we had once as his business was in a lull and clients were drying up. Our life was expensive, and we were getting further and further into debt. We considered bankruptcy, selling our over-leveraged home, even moving in with his parents. "I will give up almost anything, but I can't give up coaching," I told him. Despite how uncomfortable it was, I had to believe we were in the middle of a process, just like our kids growing up.

Rafe was also my first real client. Back in 2008, when I'd first started coaching and was in awe of my new superpowers, my beloved was at a professional crossroads. The organization he served as COO was in the midst of a leadership change, and the new leaders were taking away the executives' autonomy and authority. Rafe had picked up some consulting work on the side.

Rafe said, "I could see the opportunity. There were two roads. There was a road that was continuing the path of success for the organization, and then there was the safe and sad road to take. They chose the safe and sad road, and, for that, they really didn't need me or my colleagues. They needed somebody who was going to keep it small."

Because I could now listen differently, I became his advisor. One day he asked me a very scary question about leaving his job. My response, "Do you want to talk to your wife or your coach?"

I already know what my wife thinks. I need to talk to my coach.

MISS INDEPENDENT

ELLIE IS: two, delightful, and a handful.

I had heard raising girls was different than raising boys, and aside from the obvious, I thought, "Yeah, right." I'm the same parent, my kids should respond in the same way, don't you think?

You can keep those laughs to yourself, thanks.

Ellie and I have arrived at an impasse. She has decided that she no longer naps, and I attest that SHE NEEDS HER NAP. Perhaps to state it more clearly, I NEED HER TO NAP.

Last Monday's protest came from her crib. She took off her clothes and peed on everything. Tuesday, instead of putting her in the crib for a nap, I let her play quietly in her room. She decided to change her own diaper, and when we found her, she had removed most of the wipes from the box (and told us that she had made a monorail with the unopened packages she found in the closet!). On Wednesday, I was able to convince her that a nap was a good idea. Thursday, my parents watched the kids and were treated to an Ellie fashion show in which she removed as many items of clothing as she could from her dresser and demanded to be dressed in them. (This was after our morning in which I would dress her, and she would immediately disrobe, down to her tights!) Friday, she conceded to the nap, but hasn't had one since.

She has become exceptionally persuasive, and her language is very clear. "I DON'T WANT THAT. I DON'T LIKE THAT." Her common greeting has become, "Had a good nap," even though she just means hello because had she an actual good nap, I'd have known.

I've learned not to make the mistake of sharing information with her too far in advance, as she assumes that if I tell her we might be going to the zoo, the park, or God forbid, Disneyland, she demands that we go RIGHT NOW; time, weather, and other plans notwithstanding.

There are positive sides to her independence, too. Sometimes I find her reading to herself or singing favorite songs. Her version of the Barney classic goes, "I love me. I love me. I love Barney, I love me." Sometimes she changes the object of her affection—to shoes or Elmo. As her verbal understanding has matured, she also understands cause and effect, actions and consequences.

Me: Ellie, honey, please sit down in the cart.

Ellie: NO!

Me: Ellie, do you want to go on the carousel?

Ellie: Yes.

Me: Then, Ellie, you need to SIT DOWN. RIGHT NOW.

Ellie: Okay, Mommy.

We can then go about our business. Unfortunately, my business has become moving cereal boxes and DVDs out of her reach. She alternately dumps the cereal to eat off the floor or attempts to feed the box, in its entirety, to the dog; paradoxically, the discs are either jammed into the VCR or are placed back in their correct cases.

To summarize:

She is opinionated.

She wants to change her clothes several times a day, especially to wear more skirts.

She is demanding.

She is sweet.

She is moody.

She is talkative.

She loves shoes.

She is a girl, and she is my daughter.

On a day like today, I am religious, not just spiritually guided. I'm begging for help.

God help me through this time until we understand each other. Give me the strength to remain a mature grown-up after she has screamed at me all day. Let me have the right answer some of the time. Help me not to lose my shit the next time she empties the cupboards of toys and her drawers of all their contents after I have just put everything away.

I am grateful for my children, for every moment, for their quirks and their brilliance. Today, I am also grateful for their bedtime and a glass of wine.

"WIGGLE YOUR BUTT!"

THE NEXT EVOLUTION of my business was hatched thirty feet up a redwood tree in Northern California.

One of the many opportunities for growth in the leadership program I attended—apart from making lifelong friends, learning to reconstruct myself into the leader I truly am, and beginning to fall in love with the sound of my inner voice—was a high ropes challenge course. You've seen these a million times, parodied in movies and used in reality television competitions to show perseverance, resilience, and grit. I'd never done one before, but how hard could it be?

You'd be surprised.

Climb a ladder, use miniscule footholds to scale a tree roughly the height of a skyscraper, maneuver through a cargo net, then leap into the unknown with a metaphor for what conquering this obstacle represents for the rest of your life!

I couldn't do it.

I was stuck.

Even though I'd been loosening my grip on life, under stress, the old, familiar ways started creeping back in. For all those years leading up to me becoming a mom, I was used to doing things by myself capably, happily, and without too much distraction or interference. If I held everything I'd ever done in the past up as a mirror, I'd have convinced myself that I could do just about anything on my own.

Not anymore. Now I was stuck in a tree.

I remember how I approached it, all in my head: *Where do my hands go? What the heck am I supposed to do with the rest of my body? How can I figure this out? I'm a smart woman. I'm strong and active. How can this possibly be so difficult? How does everyone else make this look so easy?*

I knew I'd do it. With goals in place, strategies and tactics implemented, I'd get to the top fueled by courage, determination, and stubbornness like I always had. This time, it only got me twenty feet up the tree. I had at least another fifteen to go.

On that day, I wasn't just outside climbing a tree for fun, not even rescuing a stranded kitten. I was there to expand my capacity and impact in the world, starting with understanding where *I'd determined* I was limited in my resources. This tree was there for me to understand my leadership, just like the wild horses had been for the Duchess.

Up until that moment (and aside from motherhood), I thought the best way to solve problems was with my very smart and accomplished brain, to keep doing, striving, and achieving. What I learned instead: beyond my brain, my arms, feet, and legs were pretty clever, and so were the people all around me waiting and eager to help.

"Wiggle your butt, Karen!" was yelled from the forest floor below.

Huh?

One of our guides reminded me to feel the lower half of my body and see what it would do. I took a breath and reconnected to myself, beginning to climb again. Another guide offered assistance: right hand there, left foot there...asking me what else I needed.

"Make me laugh up here, people." I knew I'd have more fun if I stopped taking the challenge so seriously. Plus, I had a pretty good sense that we'd all have more fun if we did this together. All of a sudden and out of nowhere, I was part of a team. I belonged. I remembered how to trust my body, the body that had given birth to two beautiful children, the legs that love to dance, the shoulder that had healed from injuries. I accepted the advice and wisdom generously offered instead of fighting it and insisting I master the task solo.

When it was time for me to take my leap of faith, the jump from the elevated platform in the trees and gently belayed to the forest floor below, I asked for a countdown reminiscent of a circus performer attempting a death defying jump, and with a 10, 9, 8...to an audience filled with love, friendship, awe, and wonder...I soared.

I didn't know it then, but that tree and those people changed the direction of my life. I began to reintegrate the healed parts of my formerly broken self. I met more angels in the Redwoods who, just like Carrie, had a huge influence in what led to the next creation of my work—and self.

I remember two sentences from the end of that day as we shuttled back to our retreat center:

Tom Courry, now a colleague and mentor, and one of these angels on Earth who guided me as I began creating my own experiential leadership business, said, "We're a training company that does ropes courses." Those words lit me on fire.

Chris Charyk, one of the smartest guys you or I will ever meet, who became a fast friend on the drive from San Francisco to our retreat in Point Reyes, told me: "Karen, you are an extremely intelligent woman, but that is certainly not the most interesting thing about you."

I went to this retreat to become the leader I thought I was supposed to be. I left more *myself* than I had ever been before.

MARTYR MOM IS IN THE HOUSE

DESPITE MY BEST EFFORTS, from time to time I notice myself becoming someone else I never intended to be. Sometimes I'm a Martyr Mom.

Being a Martyr Mom is no fun at all. How do you know if you're a Martyr Mom?

- The Martyr Mom is overwhelmed. She sighs. A lot.

- The Martyr Mom is distracted. She cannot focus.

- She can't remember what she needed at the store, so she either buys everything or nothing.

- The Martyr Mom has difficulty making choices. There are so many to make!

- The Martyr Mom is not organized. The house is cluttered. She thinks, *Why bother cleaning if everyone's going to mess it up anyway?*

- The Martyr Mom can't find things and still spends a lot of time looking.

- The Martyr Mom makes sure the family eats (but not herself—she's always snacking or grabbing something on the run).

- The Martyr Mom coordinates the schedules of her kids but won't schedule time for herself—it's not that she can't, but she's decided what she needs to do at home is too important and can't imagine how the children will sleep if she doesn't put them to bed.

- Besides, when the Martyr Mom does have some free time, she ends up doing stuff for the house and kids anyway.

- In fact, the Martyr Mom has been in the habit of putting herself last for so long, she no longer remembers what she likes to do or how to have fun (real, honest-to-goodness fun) without her children.

- And worse, not only does she not know how to have fun, she doesn't think her having fun is important.

- The Martyr Mom is exhausted. Clearly, taking care of everyone else means she cannot take care of herself. She doesn't make time to exercise or eat well, and being so overwhelmed (all that sighing can be tiring, you know), she stays up too late thinking she's going to do something productive when the kids are finally asleep, but usually ends up watching hours of television mindlessly or playing around on the internet.

- Not a lot of what the Martyr Mom is doing feels like it's on purpose—things happen, but it's either rushed or not quite the way she wants, and she doesn't have the energy to fix it.

- The Martyr Mom spends a lot of time thinking but isn't communicating or solving problems. She's wallowing.

- The Martyr Mom has a hard time saying no, even if she's fully aware that adding one more thing to her plate means less getting done well. She sometimes gets caught up in being needed and important, and would rather please other people than take care of what is most important.

It's a vicious cycle of anxiety, this mommy martyrdom. While I realize it is self-imposed, it doesn't make it easier to break, much like my habit of using labels to find my identity. It's also an opportunity for deep healing. Getting over it, getting through it is a process, just like everything else.

COMING TOGETHER AND FALLING APART

IT WAS NOT ALL SUNSHINE AND ROSES AT HOME.

While I'd experienced a personal renaissance and awakening in Northern California, Rafe continued to struggle with our family's financial future and his obligation to solve it. We took a financial leap of faith (scarier than jumping off the platform in the Redwoods), and I enrolled in an ongoing leadership program to join a cohort that would start in the spring of 2012. One of Rafe's interim projects became a client that would sustain us for the next eight years, becoming the foundation for the exponential growth of his consulting business. We now had the financial stability to withstand more ups and downs.

I'm going to leave out details here, borrow from Dickens and say it was the best of times, it was the worst of times, and skip ahead in the story. Let it suffice to say, we were deep in our process.

Never in Rafe's mind was our marriage in jeopardy; his faith and determination glued us together. I, on the other hand, knew that we would not survive if we stayed the same; my personal transformation paved the way for his—and ours. It was a roller coaster. As I changed, my business changed with me and was renamed *Excellent Adventures*, a nod both to the experiential adventure-based work I aspired to create and lead and, of course, *Bill and Ted's Excellent Adventure*, a film released the year I graduated high school.

For all he'd done for me, us, and our family, my work was now dedicated, like a love letter, to the one person who needed it more than anyone in the world: Rafe.

MIRROR, MIRROR

JAKE IS A SENSITIVE and thoughtful soul. He gathers proof before taking risks, and it doesn't take anyone long to figure out that he won't do something until and unless he wants to. Sometimes it takes a little coaxing and cajoling, other times it is a battle of wills. You would never accuse Jake of being reckless or impulsive like you might Ellie, but he can be manipulative and stubborn. I don't say these things lightly, nor do I consider these necessarily bad traits. I'm simply more aware of what's required of me to raise my parenting game.

Four was a turning point in which I could no longer watch how he operates with wonder and distance, seeing him simply as a product of himself. At this age, I can see clearly how much he's like me. When he turns inward, unable to express himself or when he is frustrated with his lack of control over the world, I don't just see him, I see myself.

WHOA!

SIX MONTHS AFTER LEARNING how to wiggle my butt, I joined a new leadership cohort called the Caribou.

Not only did a quick Google search reveal that one of my recently introduced colleagues ran a leadership development, diversity, and inclusion program with horses(!), they were also affiliated with an equine leadership development program about twenty minutes away from my home in Los Angeles(!!). I asked to meet the founder of The Reflective Horse in Topanga Canyon, who invited me to attend an upcoming equine immersion with her herd.

A brief chronology here to refresh the memory:

Spring 2002. The crash that ended my career and took a huge chunk of my identity with it.

2002-2007. The lost years in motherhood, where I go from having no identity or idea of what to do, and learn that experience far outweighs any guidebook, to trusting myself and the process.

Fall 2007. Return to work. Realize how much it sucks because I'm still pushing/striving/trying to do it the old way, which no longer fits who I am. It does not make sense, but I've got a job to do.

Winter 2008. Recognize I can't be the only one who feels this way.

Spring 2008. Start training to be a coach. OMG, I've found my calling. Launch of karenpery.com, home of Motherhood. Reinvented.™ Help Rafe quit his job and start his own business.

Summer 2009. Start a new job while building my business. Work still sucks. Deep in the struggle.

Fall 2009. Dying inside. Something's got to change. Need to complete my training. Meet Carrie Kish. Begin to see myself differently because of the company I now keep.

Spring 2010. Rafe's business is on the upswing, and I can quit my job and focus on building my business full-time! Realize working with moms is not the thing. Don't know what is.

Winter 2010. Become a certified coach. Who'd have thought?

Spring 2011. Bored, frustrated, financially stretched. Still coaching, not thriving.

Summer 2011. Invited to join leadership program. Watch Duchess of York find herself with horses. Realize someone has *got* to be doing this.

Fall 2011. Start leadership program, fall in love with experiential learning, fall in love with self. Begin exploring ideas for new business. Realize 1) I don't have to do it on my own and 2) the person who could be doing leadership work with horses could be me.

Winter 2011. Hooray! A big client engagement secures us financially. We can keep our house!

Spring 2012. Join the Caribou and meet the horses.

You know when you do a connect-the-dots game and, all of a sudden, out of numbers and marks a picture emerges? It was like that, but the dots were my intuition, and the picture became the vision for my business and my life. At the equine leadership retreat, I experienced what my intuition had always known. All the pieces of the puzzle that broke apart now looked different and AMAZING!

Seriously, WHOA!

I didn't come for therapy or healing or even to "find myself" like the Duchess had. I had come to see for myself if equine leadership really worked because I hadn't yet embraced the truth that creating from my imagination and inspiration could be as real to me as working from a plan or from the idea of how it was "supposed to be."

On a sunny Saturday in May 2012, I got to see myself through the eyes of a horse under the guidance of the team at The Reflective Horse in Topanga Canyon. Nothing replaces learning from experience.

HOW TO TAKE CARE OF ME, BY ME

I'M GOING AWAY THIS WEEKEND. I need it. I'm very excited. And also tired. I've lost my steam. My patience has worn thin. I'm just. Plain. Burnt.

As I leave, I keep reminding Rafe how to take care of the children in my absence.

"Make sure they drink a lot of water. They can each have one juice, and that's it. If you're going to be outside, please make sure they're wearing sunscreen."

"There is plenty of milk in the refrigerator. Everyone has clean pajamas. Make sure they eat real food, not just snacks."

It goes on like this far longer than necessary. Rafe asks if I am planning to come back with a baby cow like in *City Slickers*? I don't think so, but you never know. Eventually they push me out the door.

While sitting alone the next morning enjoying the quiet, I realize that while I've become an expert at taking care of my family, I no longer remember how to take care of myself. It's not that I've entirely let myself go, and I do have most of the basics covered, but most days, I'm not what one might call "thriving." After you take care of everyone and everything, how do you take care of you?

With that in mind, I created a list.

How to Take Care of Me, by Me

1. Let it be quiet. Don't turn on the TV or computer for company.

2. Remember to feed me. Fill me up with tea.

3. Let me cook. Fill my home with wonderful smells with fresh herbs growing on the windowsill. Give me clean space in which to work. Clean up so that it is worth coming back. Eat more vegetables, make them tender with steam. Cook soups. Visit the farmer's market with no purchase in mind, but not one with carnival-like concessions.

4. Let me read. Fill my head with new ideas. Take me to far-off places, imagining a life that isn't mine.

5. Take me for walks—long walks up hills with beautiful views. Let me smell the world as it wakes up in springtime and cools in the fall. Be stronger, endure. Take the dog sometimes.

6. Fill my life with friends. Be with people who love to be with me, who find me interesting, who make me laugh and think.

(7) Love my children. Watch them grow into themselves. Laugh with them. Show them the world piece by piece. Tell them what I believe to be right and true. Read to them. Help them to blossom. Give them roots.

(8) Love my husband. Find in each other the truth of who we are. Encourage and support, still being the voice of reason. Sit closer. Hold hands. Gaze lovingly.

(9) Help me to take a break. Don't let me fill every moment with busy-ness. Teach me to meditate. Write. Be moved. Do yoga.

(10) Let me help others. Allow me to give freely my time and love.

(11) Make sure I don't forget things—birthdays, deadlines, lunches, backpacks. Use my calendar. Make lists (but only use one so they don't get lost).

(12) Help me feel pretty. Dress me well but comfortably, especially the shoes. Give me pedicures, keep my hair trimmed. Shower daily if possible. Put on my makeup. Keep me fit so that I can feel confident and happy when I see myself in pictures (and my memories are of the days well spent and not of how I wore unflattering clothes or should have been treating myself better).

(13) Help me spend my money well. Use the food we have, hire a cleaner, take tennis, ballet, yoga, time

away. Find a way to bring in an income and still be at home. Don't be afraid of not having enough.

14. Show me new things, take me to new places (especially restaurants), broaden my experience. Let me enjoy the quiet reflection in museums, especially the Getty.

15. Make sure I get enough sleep. If I'm always going to be up at 6:00, be in bed around 10:00.

16. Take me out for sushi.

17. Bring more light, warmth, and color into my home. The bedroom can be too dark. The dining room is too cold. Paint the kitchen blue, the dining room red. Install better lighting. Make the bathrooms a spa experience.

18. Remember Tlaquepaque, the ancient Aztec word meaning *the best of everything*. Do more with less.

19. Make date night fun and special.

20. Take good care of my skin, it is sensitive now. Treat it gently, moisturize.

21. If you're going to try to repair me, fix my eyes so I can see and make me stronger and more flexible so I don't feel like I'm getting old. Keep me away from the foods that make me feel bloated and edgy (and crazy in the head). See #2 and #3.

Upon returning home, I've been more consciously living to my list. I planted the herb garden and found some paint samples. I even found a great new sushi restaurant. Some days, I forget to take care of myself at all. I come back to this list and remember.

COACHING: A CONVERSATION BETWEEN RAFE AND KAREN

KAREN: You had a coach, me, throughout this process. How important was that to you?

RAFE: It was really important to me because I wasn't even thinking of these kinds of things. I was just irritated that it wasn't working. I was like *this sucks and I don't know what to do*. And I had so many other problems to figure out and solve. I wasn't even stepping back and saying *well, what if I did this?*

So, yes, it was critical because you stopped me and made me think about things that weren't on my mind. Chances are, if you are one of those people that has a really good job and you are doing pretty well, your time is pretty filled and you are probably in that same position, so having the time dedicated to talk to someone who is pushing you beyond you being like, *hey, this is my to-do list for this week,* that's good.

Sometimes the sessions are really trite, like *what do you want out of life?* And it's like *shit! I don't know! I want to be able to make it to retirement so I can enjoy some time before I die*. But that's really a terrible goal. It's nice to come up with something in the interim that feels a little better.

When you were my coach, we were talking about things that never occurred to me, and that was really important. You can be really smart and still miss a lot of things. I feel like I am good at what I do, but there are still some things I really suck at. Taking care of myself is one of them. Thinking about what is best for me is right underneath that, so how would I ever come up with a better plan than *I'll just work harder or I'll work for a bigger organization*? That's messed up.

KAREN: I know you said that many times.

RAFE: Yeah, and you know the funny thing is, and this is actually a really important thing, there's no security in your job. If you are in any job, don't think you can't get laid off or fired from your great job. So what's to be afraid of? At least with the work I do, I know if something is unraveling, and I have some forewarning. People get laid off and fired all the time, so what security really is there? Or is it simply a perceived security?

NO ONE TOLD ME

NO ONE TOLD ME that my boy was ready to grow up.

No one suggested how conflicted I'd feel when he went on his first play date without me. How much I'd want him to be independent and how much I'd miss being there to comfort him when things went wrong. No one thought about how desperately his baby sister would miss him when he didn't come home from school. How she'd cry his name, wandering the halls looking for him so they could play. No one told me how blissfully quiet my house would feel without his constant interruptions or how much I'd miss the interruptions. No one reminded me how peaceful a house seems with only one child, especially when it's the child who had to stay home to nap.

No one told me how elated I'd be when my boy arrived home. How proud I'd be that he'd gone out on his own. How I'd celebrate with him that he could have fun without his baby sister and me while secretly wishing he hadn't. No one hinted at how quickly our happiness would come crashing down when he told the story about when one of the boys called him a name and how sad he was when his mommy wasn't there to hold him and tell him it would be okay.

No one told me that he was ready for a school field trip, that he'd be fine to leave the safety of his campus with another parent, and how angry I would be that I couldn't go because baby siblings (and the mommies who have to watch them) weren't invited to tag along. No one told me that I would so obviously show my disappointment, not to my boy, but to anyone who saw me leave his classroom near tears after sending him well wishes on his big adventure. No one expected me to get over it so quickly once I accepted this was the way it was going to be.

No one told me that when my boy grew up, I'd have to grow up, too.

AN OPTIMIST FOR EVERYONE ELSE

I DON'T LIKE TO TALK ABOUT my sad stories. I can take a Pollyanna perspective on adversity, finding the silver lining to most clouds—if not immediately, then soon enough. I am a positive, big-picture thinking, unapologetically optimistic visionary—especially when it comes to other people. I see hope where others despair and take action to improve the world around me in my thoughts, beliefs, and actions. I'm a believer in the quote attributed to Rabbi Hillel, "If I am not for myself, then who will be for me? And if I am only for myself, then what am I? And if not now, when?"

Within me there is sadness, a fear that lives within a feeling of brokenness that would prefer to remain unseen and most certainly untouched. If we were talking to a therapist here, we'd probably go down the road that began when my father died in 1975, a fatal accident that took not only his life but a piece of mine as well. I was just a little girl. Developmentally, I lost a sense of trust and safety that could never be replaced regardless of how awesome my life has turned out to be.

Am I broken? Is it possible to feel like an optimist for myself? I don't know. I don't know that I'll ever know.

UNWRITTEN

IT'S THE END OF THE WORLD as we know it, and I feel sad.

I've been looking forward to it, and now that it's here, the weight of it hits me with the combined force of her twenty-six and his forty-two pounds, respectively, that my babies will be gone, and I will be alone. I have been doing this job for nearly five years. My whole life changed and is changing again, only this time, it is without the same kind of excitement and anticipation.

A couple weeks ago was Ellie's last Mommy & Me class. From here on out for her, it will be "me," no Mommy.

The next day was Jake's last day of preschool. The teachers gave gifts, there was a reception with cookies and punch. The children didn't understand what was really happening. The moms comforted each other with tissues and tears, sharing our knowing glances—our babies are growing up and there is nothing we can do about it. Might as well enjoy the cookies.

Next, Jake will go to day camp. He'll be gone almost nine hours of the day, three times a week; 135 hours of his life will be brand new. Ellie will start preschool summer camp or, as she calls it, BIG GIRL SCHOOL! Every night as she goes to bed, she asks if she gets to start school tomorrow? I tell her no, but soon. She can hardly wait! Her Tinkerbell lunch box and Dora backpack are practically packed and waiting at the door.

I am quietly dreading the silence.

It is another bittersweet parenting moment I can't escape. I am coaching their success, helping to build their confidence, hoping to provide some kind of insurance that as they try new things, they will love them and want to do more, and learn and grow as much as they can. They will be happy, independent, and successful. I will have done my job well.

If they asked me, and they certainly won't, I'd never tell them how much I'll miss them, how sad I'll be to be all by myself, and how hard it is for me to imagine our future, day by day, when I am not a part of all the good stuff.

I will simply tell each how proud I am and how much I love them.

I think that's all they really need to know.

UNWRITTEN (CONTINUED)

LIKE ELLIE, Natasha Bedingfield's song *Unwritten* came out in 2004. It described the unknowns of my life so poignantly it became my anthem, then one of Ellie's favorite songs to sing. You've never heard anything as cute as a toddler belting: "I'm just beginning, the pen's in my hand, ending unplanned... Open up the dirty window...Live your life with arms wide open. Today is where your book begins. The rest is still unwritten!"

LOST IN TRANSLATION

WE SAW A DIFFERENT SIDE of Jake on a recent vacation, one that made me see how he is developing his own point of view on relationships and communication. It is fascinating to watch a four-year-old explore his own power and authority, especially when responsible for the well-being of his baby sister. He and Ellie shared a room for the first time and, while it was quite a novelty to them, it didn't work out for us the way we hoped.

Because the room had two queen beds, we attempted to allow Ellie to sleep in one of them. Note the use of the word "attempt." Sleeping in a big girl bed was the equivalent of taking off the training wheels, and we were all a bit wobbly.

We weren't sure if she was ready, but it was a rite of passage worth pursuing.

We reminded Ellie of the story she heard many times at pre-preschool about the girl who graduates from her crib to a big girl bed. In the book, the girl has room for all her toys and she sleeps through the night without getting up a hundred times to beg her parents for one last thing. It's a classic.

The children were excited! They spoke of how they'd sing songs together, and we envisioned them peacefully drifting into slumber mid-song as we'd be sipping a glass of wine and watching the sunset from our nearby balcony. On one side, we'd hear the waves crashing on the shore and, on the other, the soft snores of our babies.

That didn't happen.

After several close calls and unexpected visits, Ellie was moved back into her crib.

From behind the closed door and the four walls of the Pack N Play, she protested.

Jake was a child transformed, a boy on a mission! He became his sister's protector and provider, her messenger, the diplomatic envoy serving to relay information between her and us. He was her link. Her hero. He took it all very seriously.

We heard the door open, followed by the padding of Jake's little feet on their way to find us now guzzling our glasses of wine and wishing that the ocean sounds would muffle the racket of our beloved children not sleeping.

Jake: Mommy, Daddy, Ellie says she wants to sleep in the big girl bed.

Daddy: But Jake, we tried, and Ellie's just not ready for the big girl bed. She doesn't understand that she can't keep getting up and leaving. She has to sleep in her crib.

Jake: But she really wants the big girl bed.

Daddy: Sorry, Jakey, Ellie's not ready for the big bed yet. She's still a baby, and she's going to have to sleep in the crib so we can all be rested for tomorrow.

Jake: Oh. Okay.

He slowly walked back to their room, considering the weight of what he'd been told, balanced against his sister's desires.

We heard him pause at the door to report back to her: "Ellie, Daddy says you're a baby. You're sleeping in the crib."

EQUINE EMPOWERMENT

IMMERSED IN THE BEAUTY of Topanga Canyon and led by the guides at The Reflective Horse, we observed the herd. Seeing how they interacted as individuals and in a group dynamic, we were asked to make assumptions—if this were a corporation, what are their roles? What do you see? Who are you drawn to? What might be happening here?

I watched one horse that seemed young and filled with energy and determination. It reminded me of myself everywhere I worked in my twenties and early thirties. Seeing how the other horses responded, I had an immediate sense of how my impact might not have been what I'd intended (and why I'd received some rough evaluations). This was going to get interesting.

Being prey animals, horses are incredibly sensitive to their environment, constantly assessing and evaluating their safety. Their sensitivity is a superpower, and they are extraordinary partners when it comes to developing emotional range, discovering leadership abilities, and healing. *(Sensitivity as a strength? Tell me more, my new best friends.)* To be in relationship with a horse requires honest communication. They sense what we, as humans and predators, feel before we even put words to our feelings. It is imperative they know if they are safe or in danger. Are you honest with yourself? Do you act like you're not afraid when you are? Horses innately sense the feelings beyond the words. Given they know the difference between a hungry mountain lion and one that's full, they can certainly sense if you're not telling the whole truth.

What words matched my feelings? Nervous, excited, curious, and anxious. I am comfortable around animals and trusted the team and the program, even while saying to myself, "Oh my God, these are giant animals, and I'm a tiny human, what am I thinking?!" For the opportunity to interact with these magnificent beings, I was willing to be real. After the fall leadership retreat, I'd begun to practice being okay with not having it all together and being accepted just as I am without having to do more or prove anything. It was still fresh.

Though I didn't really know how to say hello to a horse, I knew I wanted to be as calm and open as possible. It was thrilling! The horses were also calm, present, grounded, and available. I approached the horses. They chewed on my watch. We were close to each other. I stood with them, in awe of the connection, and looked at the lead mare, Java.

We stood shoulder to shoulder, the mare and I, as if old friends connecting over a cup of tea.

This sense of pure connection was unfamiliar, and in my uncertainty, I started questioning, "What do I do? What am I here to learn?" When I left my heart and started analyzing the moment, Java walked away. *What?* When I was indecisive and trying to figure out whatever it was I was "supposed" to be learning from the horses, they disconnected from me. When I was present, we were connected. When I wasn't clearly communicating, the horse left. When we were engaged and I trusted my instinct, I was able to lead and the horse followed me. When I started to worry and waiver, the horse went the other way. When I felt confident, playful, and open—relating to the herd as I would my dogs—it was easy. I was immediately aware of the developmental work I still had to do.

As a leader, I am hard to follow when I worry and doubt. It is hard for me to lead when I'm not clear about what I want.

Where does this show up? All the time. Making dinner, making plans. I'm so worried and concerned about taking care of others that I take myself out of the picture. I disappear. Maybe it's in the service of others, but underneath is a belief and a sense that I don't really trust my instincts or my wants. The horse knows. My beliefs and intentions are powerful.

I'd never before received such precise, deep, and immediate insights into my impact. Receiving feedback from a horse is different than your typical 360-degree evaluation. Unlike other reviews, the horse in front of you is not your boss or your client, can't fire you, and won't determine your next raise or promotion. The horse is not there to buy anything you're trying to sell.

The equine leadership program was perfectly timed. I needed to see my Redwood-tree inspired leadership development training concepts in action to believe it. I wanted confirmation that leaders could benefit from working with horses in as meaningful ways as I'd seen with the kids at the Riding Center all those years ago and that it wasn't the magic of television with Martha Beck and the Duchess. I had to know that my creative ideas could be as impactful as my well-thought out plans. If I couldn't see how *I* could change through experiential learning, there was no way I'd be able to lead others down the same path. The horses gave me feedback I desperately needed to hear. The experience gave me the confidence and courage to take the next step in building my dream business and to know that my dream was possible. With horses as my teachers, I could see my blind spots, and I was able to change. When I changed, *everything* changed.

DESERVING

MY DEAR SWEET JAKE,

You are seven and a half now.

Early last week, you did something that wasn't planned or exactly what I had hoped. You knew it was wrong, and you felt terrible—so much so that there was some reward or indulgence *you decided you didn't deserve to have* as a result of your behavior.

The way you took it to heart broke mine. I explained as best as I could that you deserved plenty of good things, but perhaps this misstep hadn't earned you any extra arbitrary points in the game of life. It's not that I'm trying to spare you the details, believe me. It was such a small thing that a week later neither of us remembers what happened. And though I'm sure you've forgotten the rest, I can't let the *deserving* part go.

My child, you deserve the world. You deserve to be loved and appreciated. You deserve loyal friends and a warm bed in which you'll sleep at night to have the sweetest of dreams. You deserve experiences that engage and inspire you to learn more and to be more. You deserve kindness and opportunities.

You deserve the best of all things because that's what you are. You are seven, a little kid. (A little kid with an old soul.)

Last week, while you were berating yourself for something totally inconsequential, I was watching you grow. At teacher conferences, I learned that when other kids are having a hard time in your class, your teacher rearranges the desks so that you can sit next to kids who need a little extra support. You are such an important part of the classroom because you are so kind and helpful. A few days later at karate, you were pushing yourself to do something I can't even imagine doing myself—something like a million squats, push-ups, leg raises, and sit-ups (or at least that's what it looked like from the bench). You got frustrated. You had to leave the mat. You collected yourself and pushed harder. When the young assistant asked the teacher why you kept going, the teacher knew: you kept going because you wanted to. These things are not academic subjects. They are not skills that can be taught. This is who you are.

A few days after that, you saw something and were so intrigued, I offered you my camera to capture the moment. I expected you to take the camera with great reverence and then to fill the card with things that mattered only to you.

You took one photo. It was of me.

When it comes to deserving, I'm not quite sure what I did right to deserve the privilege of being your mom, but I'm so glad I did.

Love,

Mommy

THE FOG

I HEARD A STORY about a woman who set out to swim the Catalina Channel. She quit only a half-mile from shore because she couldn't see it past the fog. Determined after this near success, she later completed the swim, not only becoming the first woman to do so but also setting a new record.

After the story, I thought about my own goals. Where was my fog? Oh yeah, I have two young children. When someone has a bad day, we all have a bad day.

I begin to question if the kids are really my fog or if they're just part of the noise.

My life has always had noise. It feels like hearing the constant sound of bees buzzing near a hive, only it's in my head. Sometimes I can't focus. The wondering stops me from actually doing. *Am I doing enough? Am I enough?*

It's worse in some rooms than others. When the actual noisy people are quietly occupied, the noise gets louder. It's probably loudest in the kitchen. *It's a mess. What's for dinner? How am I going to get through a trip to the store without someone melting down? Is this food going to waste? How can I be up for four hours and still not have time to feed us all a decent breakfast before Jake goes to school? What's this sticky stuff on the floor? Why can't Daisy wipe her feet before coming into the house? Why does Ellie have to empty the drawers all the time? Why didn't we put more safety locks on the cabinets? Where did we put the extra ones? She can't get to the dangerous stuff, do we really need to put safety locks on the cabinets if she's going to outgrow this phase in a few months? I should be drinking more water. How am I going to lose weight if I don't drink enough water? Why can't I find a clean cup? How old does Jake have to be to start doing chores so I don't always have to empty the dishwasher? Is it already time to pick Jake up? Is it already 3:00 and I haven't had lunch? Did I even have breakfast? What am I doing? What's that smell?*

Days go on, some are better, others worse. It's hard, this life of a stay-at-home mom, but I've learned to like it and see it's a good fit for me, even if I do question everything constantly. *Do I even know what my goals are? How does one quantify the goal of having happy, well-adjusted children? Can I be a good mother if I can't figure out what I want for myself and how to get there?* I am trapped. I am tired. I am distracted. I can't stay awake. I can't stay asleep. I am impatient. I am sad. I feel like an utter and complete failure. *How am I going to lose weight if I can't get a grip? How can I be a good mother if I can't even take care of myself?*

I find myself out running errands and unable to make decisions, unable to cope with the crowds, the parking, the stores, the choices, the consequences, and I stop. I go home. I cry. Rafe feeds the kids and takes them upstairs for their bath. I feel terrible. Hopeless. *Is this anxiety? Depression? This isn't me anymore.*

I start making better choices, and the fog starts to lift. I am able to focus. I feel like I'm accomplishing things. I am happier. I am nicer. I am able to see the beauty in my life and not just the flaws. I am aware of when I need to eat and what will make me feel better. I'm not 100%—there is no way I'd skip the cupcakes I baked for my baby girl's birthday party, but I can have one of them instead of four (or six!). I skip the M&M's. I don't miss them. I don't really want them. I don't feel so bad.

As it turns out, my children aren't the fog, they're just part of the noise. It was me all along. I'm fine with the noise, not the ongoing funk. Apparently, I needed the noise to get loud enough before the fog could lift.

UNLIKELY PAIR

THE EQUINE RETREAT I ATTENDED was in May. In June, I was in another forest at another retreat, this time in Sonoma, California. My partner Gary and I had ten minutes to create and co-lead our first experiential workshop, having never created anything together, also having met in person just days before. Oh, and we were going to be leading this experiential workshop on another high ropes challenge course (with no way to complete this challenge solo), about thirty feet up in the trees, and Gary was afraid of heights.

Gary and I met in March of 2012 when I joined the Caribou leadership tribe. We connected on Facebook first and got to know each other as we worked on weekly homework assignments. We connected like magnets. If we were both interested in a topic, we dug in and got dirty. We pushed each other, though if you ask him, he'd tell you I was the only pushy one. We had to test if what we were learning was real and practical, so we took our homework into day-to-day challenges. Conveniently and concurrently, Gary and his wife, Kanako, had left Vancouver and were living in Hawaii for three months. Living in Hawaii for a summer was a dream of mine, and they were doing it. Without knowing him, I knew I'd like him.

In a group of twenty-four leaders, we were constantly *randomly* paired for exercises or we'd end up sitting next to each other, forced to interact. I liked Gary as a person, the guy I'd studied with online, but in person, there wasn't much *there* there.

I have a decent idea why we nearly missed our connection. Here's who we were at the time:

June 2012 Gary Mahler: floaty, calm, serene, and aloof. His body was in the room, but his mind was somewhere else. He seemed disinterested and cool. Above it all. He was quiet and never spoke his mind; he was nothing like the guy I knew online who was pushing me so we could both learn more.

June 2012 Karen Pery: guns blazing, bull in a china shop, hungry for knowledge, change, transformation, impact, and power all at once; a mix of confidence, arrogance, and insecurity. The kind and curious person I was over email was lost in person as I acted out how I thought I was supposed to be. You'd never really know *me* because the real me was too messy, and you didn't get to see that part. I was exhausting.

A few notes about how Gary and I have worked since the very beginning:

(1) It's never only "work." Our first conversations were a hybrid of leadership theory mixed with practical explorations like *where do you find the best shave ice on the North Shore of Oahu, and have you tried the kiawe grilled chicken in the parking lot next to the market in Haleiwa? I think the truck is only there on Saturdays, but definitely*

go if you can. We encouraged and supported each other to take risks and were there to talk about what happened when things worked and when they didn't.

(2) We don't think like most people do, but we do think alike. When we are passionate, focused, and fascinated, we are ALL IN, and when we found the topics we wanted to discuss with our peers met mostly with silence, we took ourselves offline to help each other. This continues to be true. We have always had each other's back, 100%-100%.

(3) We know how unique and extraordinary our relationship is. We take care of each other and our work. Nothing gets done if we are not good with ourselves and/or with each other. Presence is golden. This is so important that we build it into our retreats so others can learn how to do and BE like this. Accepting and loving the people you are with for who they are, exactly as they are, is a radical act. Gary taught me that.

Given all I've just described, you might imagine sparks flying, fireworks, and a parade when we finally met in person, that we'd have instant chemistry and there would be no question we'd do something big together.

If you thought that, you would be wrong.

Meeting in person was actually a bit of a letdown. (At least for me. Sorry, Gare Bear.) The Gary I met in person was someone I wrote off and decided I didn't need to impress, a blessing in disguise. If I'd felt like I had to prove myself to him, he would not have known the real me; he would have been put off by my pretense and been especially guarded. In a different situation, I would have tried to prove my worth and significance out of fear. I would have kept him at a distance because of how deeply I judged myself and never felt I measured up.

I would have found him distant and cold (because, as I would later find out, Gary would have disappeared unless you were willing and able to earn his love and respect, and then he might let down his guard a millimeter) and instead looked for someone more like me who I was sure would make something happen.

If we had been anything but real with each other, we would have never created the most transformational beach party in the world.

THIS IS WHAT IT LOOKS LIKE… WHEN I AM FALLING APART

IT HAPPENS SLOWLY. IT BUILDS. Things will be going along just fine, and then they aren't. Nothing big, but the little things start feeling bigger.

I don't want to do anything. It's not that I can't, I just can't conceive of why I might do anything when it is so easy to *not* do anything. I sit. I find distractions. I wallow.

I panic about the things I cannot control. I obsess about the things about which I have taken no action.

I stop planning ahead. I don't want to be around people when I feel this way. I don't even want to be left with my own thoughts much less those of someone else.

I withdraw.

If I could, I would curl up in my bed and cry. Not about anything in particular, but simply to do something of my own accord. Something where I am not needed by anyone else. Something totally self-indulgent. I wish I could find something else more self-indulgent to do, but I am bound by duty. I simply can't. This is all I can muster.

I can't go for a long walk with Ellie and Daisy. Ellie will scream. I will carry her. I'll dislocate my other shoulder.

Jake is crying at school again. I can't make him stop. I leave him in tears. I try to move on, but I'm left with the image of my boy desperate for me. I feel I've failed him. I feel I've failed myself. I don't know what to do. I am angry.

Rafe is going away again because he can...because he should. I should go away, too. Where would I go? What would I do?

I look for jobs trying to find the answers. We will have two children in private school. It is expensive. I need to work. I need to work and still be home for them. I need to contribute, and I don't know how. I am afraid to sacrifice being a good mom for having to work, and I have to work. I know change is coming, and there is nothing I can do to stop this train now that it's left the station.

I am checked out. Disengaged. Lost.

If I were not me, I would tell me to just do something. Anything to feel a sense of accomplishment. Set a goal and do it, even if it is just taking out the trash. *Is accomplishment a drug, and am I addicted?*

Instead, I start and stop, start and stop. Doing a little of something that results in nothing. I am stuck, a pendulum swinging back and forth, not getting anywhere.

Sometimes I find myself sitting at the computer, not knowing why. I am searching for something but nothing in particular. Blogs, games, news, eBay, whatever it is, it is not My Life Right Now. Everything feels out of control, so I escape into distractions. Anything to numb myself. I know it's all in my head, and I can't escape my thoughts, so I create ways to disconnect. Not thinking about myself becomes the most worthwhile pursuit I can manage.

I need to clean the house for the holiday. But it seems pointless to clean, day in and day out. The kids spill juice, and it marks the rug. Playdough is embedded along with wax, dog hair, and God only knows what else. The dog tracks in dirt, making mud on the carpet from the overflow of the kids' bath. I need to clean the car, too. The vacuums work but not as well as what I need. I need something professional. I should hire professionals. I should be a professional, then we could hire more professionals.

I am not a professional homemaker, housewife, or mother, but if pressed to fill out my "occupation," technically, to the rest of the world, that's what I am. I am contributing to the betterment of society by raising my children. A lot of days, I feel like a hack; borrowing a programming definition, I am an inelegant solution to a temporary problem, only the problem is being a good wife and mother, and it is by no means temporary.

I used to spend my time better, but there used to be less on my mind. I go from feeling like I have it all together to feeling like I've been floundering since I left my full-time paid job. Sometimes I wish I wasn't able to stay home. If I always had to work, I wouldn't now have to figure out how to rub two sticks together to make a new career. I could still be a good mom and raise great kids, a lot of parents do, but this was our decision, as it is to send these children to private school, so I have to work and still be the primary caregiver. I don't know how to start over.

I am afraid I will fail. I will fail at figuring out how to live my dream and will end up doing the kind of work that feels like a prison sentence. I am afraid that the sacrifice will be too much and that the children won't be raised well enough. I am afraid I will lose myself and be absent to my children. I am afraid that even when I'm present, I am absent.

Sometimes I wish I had already failed so that I could get over it and move on.

As I was thinking this, Ellie discovered how amazing it is that we all have belly buttons. For a moment, lost in her wonder, everything felt good and possible again.

ACCOMPLISHMENT JUNKIE, PART 2

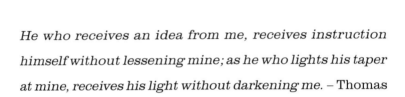

He who receives an idea from me, receives instruction himself without lessening mine; as he who lights his taper at mine, receives his light without darkening me. – Thomas Jefferson via Malcolm Gladwell in *What the Dog Saw and Other Adventures*

NORMALLY, I WOULDN'T KEEP the comments from a blog post, but what happened here inspired me and showed me I'm not the only one struggling to remember the best of myself in the fog of motherhood. I might be a voice for something.

(1) I think you've got it. And you know, it seems like such a statement of the obvious and yet, it is actually a really valid insight that had never occurred to me (nor had ever been mentioned to me before): that really is a valid theory about why mommies compete. Like you, I too am driven and accomplishment-oriented. I need that. And to

get it, I often seek it outside the home. I worry, sometimes, that it means I'm away too much. And yet I am really a SAHM. Struggle and balance.

(2) I want my report card, dammit! That is what makes motherhood so hard for the achievers, the list-makers (guilty!). I need to get to a place where it feels like an accomplishment if I did nothing but spend time with my little guy that day.

(3) It IS a struggle and a balance. I went back to work after 3 months of maternity leave and felt relief. I can say with certainty that YOU are the one that is doing the hardest job ever. YOU DESERVE A RAISE and straight A's!!!

(4) I think the only things that make us feel validated as mothers are: 1) having another mother say, "I know" without hearing a word from you, 2) having your babies come only to you when they need comforting. Have a margarita with an extra shot of tequila on me b/c, woman, I could never do your job!

(5) I can totally relate to this. I am a checklist person, too. Just when I think I've accomplished something and made strides as a mother, some new unknown just comes crashing in to knock me down.

(6) Your post totally resonates with me. I feel torn between the woman I was and the woman I am becoming…

(7) I really resonated with this post because I too am torn between the woman I once was pre-child and the woman I am becoming with child.

(8) Yup yup yup. (Just nodding my head here.)

(9) You are an amazing woman! I have all the respect in the world for the sacrifices you are making for your children! Keep setting those goals, girl! I feel certain you will reach every one of them!

FLEUR DE SEL CARAMEL, MY MARE, MY MIRROR

HORSES ARE EMOTIONAL MIRRORS TO HUMANS.

I fell for Fleur de Sel Caramel hard and fast like when I met Rafe. Only a few times in my life have I felt that immediate connection—first Rafe, then Carrie, then online with Gary—so when it happened with Fleur, I trusted that sense of knowing, that fast lightning bolt of a yes.

We rescued Fleur in October 2012 and sent her to live with her trainer Angi (before she was Fleur, she was known as Angi's Baby), until she's ready to come home to us. And when will she be ready? I have no idea.

Fleur is a smart little mare. She learns quickly and is eager to please. She wants to work with you, she's got an incredibly sweet disposition, but bottom line—it's hard for her to trust.

I watch Fleur with Angi, and she breaks my heart in pieces.

You can see how tense she is. I asked Angi the other day if horses can actually have anxiety attacks, hyperventilate, and faint. Her worried brow, her eyes frozen wide and still, her jaw clenched, her breathing tense and deliberate with an anticipation that *something* will happen. She holds it all in until she doesn't—she either relaxes, receptive and ready to go, or begins to buck like a bronco at a rodeo, acting as if she's about to die. (One time this happened when Fleur stepped on a crunchy leaf—it may as well have been the end of the world.)

It's Angi's job to help Fleur trust herself to be okay in a world that is unpredictable. It's no small task. Not for Fleur, not for anyone.

I tell Angi we'll wait as long as it takes. While I'm eager to have Fleur join us near home where she'll one day share a pasture with a delightful herd of equine companions, I won't rush her. I know what it's like to be sensitive. I know what it's like to fear for safety, even when unthreatened. I know what it's like to hold it all in, and I know what it's like to explode from the pressure of it. I know what it's like not to trust even the most gentle and generous, and I know how hard it is to simply receive the love that surrounds you.

She is my horse, and I am her person. I love her like no other. Looking at pictures of us together, Rafe says we even stand alike. I don't know when she'll come home to us, but I know she will. Together we will grow more than we would alone.

Fleur is my angel, and I am hers.

Note to the reader: There's no way I could've known (until I did) that had it not been for Fleur and our connection, and my commitment to helping her be the very best horse she can be, we wouldn't have our ranch now. If she were easy (a Jake of a horse), we would have brought her home immediately and ended up with two horses, but because she is more of an Ellie, she needed more time and focused attention. In doing whatever it took to help her realize her potential, we developed a relationship with Angi that would lead to our partnering together and the expansion of Wrong Turn Ranch.

HOPES & DREAMS

3:21 P.M., THE CAR.

"How was your first day of school?!"

"Great!"

"What's awesome about third grade?"

"Everything!"

"Any homework today?"

Eyes rolling. "Yeah, mom. It's <u>T</u>hird <u>G</u>rade. *Of course* I have homework already. And so do you...."

Perplexed, concerned about looming deadlines for what is already in the queue and what is now to be added, she answers, "Really? Me? What homework do I *have to do* for you today?"

Confidently and said with the assurance that this was, indeed, the smallest task in the entire known world, "Yeah. You have to write about your hopes and dreams for me."

With tears welling briefly and the slightest catch in her voice, "Oh. I think I can do that."

"And it has to fit in this outline of a heart on this sheet of paper."

I completed my assignment. A few of my words fill a heart that will hang on the wall of a new classroom; the rest have overflowed onto my screen.

I wish for you to be curious about what it is you are being told and taught. I hope you will be interested, even passionate, about things you love and things that trouble you so much that you devote your time and energy to making a difference, making what is good better, and making what is hard easier. I wish for you to question and to answer, and to raise your hand to ask, accepting that right isn't always right or wrong, wrong. My hope is that you will embrace a spiritual tradition that is resonant and meaningful, and that knowing and living our history and understanding our people will ground and connect you to something greater; that you will honor this, that the lessons will give you perspective and humility when it serves you and a sense of humor when it doesn't. I wish that your days are filled with laughter, that you find in yourself the resolve to strive for mastery and accept adequacy and imperfection as well. My hope is that you will learn from wherever you find yourself. I wish for your eyes to see so much beauty that you are compelled to create, and that it comes effortlessly from the endless universe of your imagination. I hope that you will continue to confide in me, to celebrate and dream with me, and to hold my hand even though you're old enough to not want to anymore. My dream is that you will walk your path with confidence knowing that who and what you are is amazing, that you will one day (and every day) see in my eyes the great awe and wonder with which I see you and hold you in my heart and have since the day you were born. My hope is that you will always be cherished and loved by your friends and that you will offer and receive friendship as a gift and give it freely without fear of being hurt. My hope and dream is that you will hope and dream, too.

EXCELLENT ADVENTURES: A CONVERSATION BETWEEN RAFE AND KAREN (CONTINUED)

KAREN: There's an activity in this class I'm teaching. You ask a room full of people what your dream is, not what your plan is or how you are going to do it, you actually ask: "What's your dream without saying how it's going to happen? What would be fun?"

RAFE: What is your happy place?

KAREN: Yes.

RAFE: That was a good one.

KAREN: When I play that game, all sorts of things come out of my mouth.

RAFE: Like what?

KAREN: Well, for a while I wanted to live in Paris. Another one of my dreams is to be able to ride Fleur whenever I want.

RAFE: Yeah, that's a good one. You actually could now.

KAREN: Now, what's your dream?

RAFE: Well, I have one dominating dream, and I just talked about it last night. I want to saddle up and ride free as far as I can, and it would all be our land.

KAREN: I am seriously dreaming about going to surf camp for a week. I think that would be cool.

RAFE: Well, I have several side dreams that are part of that. I want to continue living our life with Angi and Seth and supporting their training, which I think is just incredible. I want our kids to experience that in life. And I want to bring people to it. Have barbeques and drink wine and be with the horses.

It would be great for someone who wouldn't say yes to coaching, they may say yes to hanging out with our horses. I believe your model of experiential leadership is good because a lot of people would say no to coaching, but they will say yes to surfing or ropes course or wave runners or whatever it is... or horses.

I bet I could get people to come out. "Hey, we are going to ride all day, we are going to camp out, we are going to ride back, and then we are going to barbeque and drink wine and tell stories about what happened."

KAREN: And maybe ask the question about how this is important in your life.

RAFE: Yes, or like what's missing? Then we can all sit around the campfire and cry.

I'LL DO ANYTHING

SHE WALKED TENDERLY TOWARD THE STAIRS, conducting a mental inventory of the freezer and considering what would make the best ice pack for the growing bump on her knee. She paused to scratch the puppy's belly. "Absolutely, 100% worth it, no question," she thought to herself as she smiled at her sweet young companion. "I'd do anything for him."

The latest "anything" she was thinking about was the dive she took on the garage floor earlier in the day, simultaneously banging her face against the side of her car and both knees on the hard cement while successfully grabbing the puppy's collar and keeping him from running into the street. The bruised knees told of a much happier story than most of the alternatives she imagined.

Her head-on collision with her Volvo's door was the last in a series of unfortunate events that week. The day before, she'd succumbed to a bout of food poisoning she attributed to her food court lunch, a quick bite between getting the kids' haircuts and sturdy new shoes for summer camp. She was thankful that only she was ill, not her children, thankful that her fever broke before she crawled into bed, which eased her fears of getting much worse before she was any better. Who would she call if she found herself needing to go to the ER in the middle of the night with all of the adults in her family out of town? Who would come to care for two kids, one of whom could at any moment be on the verge of an ER visit with the same symptoms, and two dogs, one of whom she'd tripped over in the night, which had her researching orthopedists, hoping the relentless soreness in her shoulder wasn't going to lead to surgery? No one else could do this. It had to be her.

She sat on the kitchen floor and wept, everything hurting at once. Wedged between the recycling bin and the cupboard, she found herself sobbing and allowed the tears to flow. In her mind, she asked the Universe, "WHAT ARE YOU TRYING TO TELL ME?! Why do I keep ending up on the floor? What am I supposed to see from here?" No answers came. The puppy retreated to his crate, and her daughter breezed by, blowing kisses and sending wishes that mommy would feel better soon.

The kids were snug in their beds, their next day's outfits chosen and lunches packed, a huge win considering the day—and week—she'd had. Her daughter had tucked herself in while her brother got the first bedtime cuddle, which had apparently taken too long.

"I didn't think you'd come."

"Have I ever not come?" the woman replied without a breath of defense or exasperation. With at least ten kisses, hugs, and promises of eternal love and devotion, the little girl said goodnight. Gently closing the door behind her and picking up one stray sock in the hall, the woman thought to herself with a loving and knowing sigh, "I'd do anything for that child."

She peeked into her son's room, noticing the silhouettes of partly formed Lego statues against the pale blue walls. It seemed that the boy had fallen asleep the second his head had hit the pillow. The toddler who had moved into that room eight years ago would be finishing the third grade in a matter of days. The woman found herself saying to anyone who would listen (mostly her friends with children the same age and in the same state of disbelief), "I can't believe I'm going to be the mother of a fourth grader. I remember fourth grade." The thought occurred again, what she'd do for her boy. Anything.

A text of encouragement to her husband—out of town and needing to hear just the right words to support a difficult decision. Anything. What she'd do if asked, what she'd do if needed, what she'd do if called upon and could not conceive of saying no. Anything.

Sitting down in front of the television with a popsicle for dinner and a bag of frozen peas numbing her aches, she wondered how it was that she would do anything for someone else but struggled so much to define the anything she would do for herself with as much passion, devotion, and urgency. Something had to change.

WHAT I KNOW ABOUT THE PAST, PRESENT, AND FUTURE

I CAN SUM UP WHAT I KNOW about the past, present, and future in a few words. You can't change the past. It's over. You are here now. Breathe. The rest will happen.

The past is tricky. Events and circumstances may be over, but emotional investments and entanglements linger and permeate the present and future. When we say, "It's over," what does it take to let go so we can move forward? Remaining attached to the past is like having a house burn down and then sifting through the ashes trying to rebuild it. It doesn't work, no matter how hard you try.

Emotional loss—one in which your idea of yourself has changed because of changes in your body, career, health, fertility, family, friendships, relationships, athletic abilities, or whatever once seemed to matter more than anything else but is now gone—can affect you as deeply as the physical loss of a loved one and may need to be grieved as honestly and deliberately.

I've written a lot about the time when I didn't know who I was. Motherhood did not mesh with my ideas about myself; I'd invested a lot of time telling myself a story about the necessity of proving myself, one in which I was convinced that I was only the sum of what I had accomplished. I felt lost when I became a mother because I wasn't *doing* anything else and I no longer had anything to prove.

It was a phase. It lasted quite a while, but it was only a phase. And now it's over.

It's hard for me to remember my old self. One day, I realized that the great big story I'd written about myself was fiction. I see myself differently now. I am multitudes. I am not defined by who employs me, how educated I am, how much I earn, what I weigh, what size I wear, who I love, or how I give.

To arrive at that destination, I had to let go of the past. I needed to honor the time and commitment I'd given to my career and acknowledge the impact I made. I felt sadness remembering how strong, smart, powerful, and important I had felt when I thought I was in control. I missed that part of my life. I didn't know how to feel those things without working and doing something. I had to mourn the life I'd left behind and accept that it was over in order to move forward. When I was able to see that those were *parts* of my life and not my whole life, my story changed.

Trying to put myself back in the past was like watching Ellie trying to shove her feet into the pink patent leather Mary Janes she wore when she learned to walk at eleven months old. They do not fit. My old story no longer fit when I realized I outgrew it.

You are here now. Breathe. The rest will happen.

THE LOOK

DO YOU EVER CATCH A REFLECTION, wondering who that woman is, and realize it's you?

Do you wonder what others see when they see you? What do your friends/kids/family see? When you picture the face of a loved one, do they look happy and joyful or sour and a little put out? Photos capture these great moments—celebrations, family fun, even a vacation—but the look on my face says *it's not so great.* When not posing for the camera, I look more than a bit irritated. If it only happened once, I'd think it an anomaly caught on film. Instead, it appears that I am chronically disappointed.

When I see pictures of myself, there are things that always find my focus. How does my hair look? Is it a good length? Can I get away with washing it less? What about my arms? My belly? Is it a flattering outfit? I see these snapshots for what they are—a moment captured in time—and also a reflection of who I am and what I am thinking.

Am I always tired? Worried? Expecting something bad to happen? Yes, unfortunately, most of the time I am. I think these are ongoing conditions of motherhood. I don't know who I would be if I wasn't always worried about something.

I can easily change my hair or lipstick. I can lose a few pounds and do more crunches. I can get rid of those unflattering pants and see-through blouses. I can get a little more sleep. But how do I drop the attitude? Where can I get a contentment upgrade? I'd like to shed a bit of seriousness and find a reserve of fun. And while I'm at it, I'll take a little more amazement and an extra dose of wonder, too.

Here is what I am pondering:

1. Both my kids will be in school soon, and I will have some free time on my hands. (This makes me alternately cheerful and sullen.)

2. Same children will be concurrently enrolled in fancy, private schools because we're hell-bent on giving them the best education we can. (It was one thing for one kid to be in an expensive school but another altogether to have them both doing it at the same time. And did I mention that it will be for the next decade?)

What you don't know is that this week marks the fifth anniversary of my last day of paid employment. Probably not entirely coincidentally, I recently made the connection between not working and missing a sense of accomplishment that tends to come with a paycheck and not with diaper changes and sippy cup refills. Not saying that the latter is not as worthwhile as the former, but as a full-time occupation, it is just not the same.

If you put the pieces together like I did, you'd see that maybe it is time to dust off the old résumé and start networking again. I'm ready. It's taken me a full five years to realize that while I don't want to do exactly what it was I did before I left to have Jake (technically, to sit on my ever-growing behind for three months waiting for Jake to be born, since my doctor insisted that my unborn child needed me more than my employer did), I think I could be very effective doing a version of what I used to do, from home, part-time. (I hope.)

THE BIRTH OF INTO THE FIRE

IMAGINE THIS: you're in a room of twenty-four people and you each have thirty seconds to pitch your dream project to each other. You've boiled your life's work down to a few bullet points on a Post-it note. It's not a room of sharks, and you're not looking for an investor or mentor—you're looking to meet a project partner to create something inspired by your shared vision.

I improvised and developed a pitch for leaders to attend circus school. "Get out of the three-ring circus of your life literally by learning to fly on a trapeze!"

With music blasting in a process that felt a lot like musical chairs, we entered into a flurried frenzy of people and ideas. A few involved adventures, but only one resonated: a weeklong workshop in Hawaii teaching leaders to create a "business at peace."

And who was the brilliant mind behind this idea? Gary. Of course it was Gary. The music stopped, and at the end of the round, it was time to match up and find your chair—I mean partner.

Out of the corner of my eye and across the room, I saw the green t-shirt containing the one and only person I wanted to create with—Gary Mahler. He says my intensity parted the crowd like Moses and the Red Sea. I asked Gary to be my partner before anyone else could. He said yes. (He'd tell you I never gave him a chance to say no.)

So here we were: two people, who knew each other a little, given an incredible and insane task of creating a brand-new experiential workshop for seven to ten people to be designed, planned, executed, filmed, and critiqued before our next leadership retreat. In a little over two months, we would build, bond, and lead a project. At minimum, it was a required homework assignment; at its heart, it could change lives, starting with ours.

We had twenty minutes to learn everything we could about each other. What did we have in common, and what did our circus and Hawaii projects have in common? We couldn't use either for our new project. We had to collaborate on something original, and partnership was the avenue to exponential creativity! Included in our task: representing who we were and why we were here together on this planet at this moment in history.

No pressure, right?

As Gary and I spoke, it was as though we were meeting mirror images. In our past lives, we were both stressed-out Type A people. Neither of us ever liked looking bad, and on occasion we could both have been described as controlling. We had each been trapped feeling like our value as humans was derived from what we could accomplish or produce.

We'd both had success professionally and knew that no amount of money or success could heal a shattered heart because it hadn't for us. We felt like machines that were rewarded for getting things done, and we knew others felt like this, too. We wanted to bring more awareness into how we—and others—felt, since robots don't know how to feel.

We talked about what inspired us and the contrasts in our lives: numbness vs. aliveness; feeling human or feeling like a machine designed to produce and achieve; being light or being serious; having space to create or forcing creativity through false urgency.

Gary had a perspective that expanded mine. He saw what I couldn't yet articulate—a need to discover what it means to become alive (it's what he's known for). At that time, my experiential leadership concept was to immerse people in fun, new experiences where, aside from making new memories, they would discover something new about themselves and become better leaders. When you realize that you are more than you thought you were (and not a getting-things-done-machine), you have new opportunities and choices to make.

We decided our project would give people a vacation in a day because everyone we knew needed one. We'd give them space to simply be themselves, to try things they'd never done (like you could in Hawaii), take risks, and very likely fail (like you might at Circus School), but you'd laugh at yourself while failing. We wanted people to feel alive. We felt like people were living lives of habit, doing what they did by default—because that's what we'd done.

Our project had to be all the things—a new experience, new people, outdoors, somewhat risky, with periods of stillness and reflection. In essence, we wanted to see what happened to people (leaders) when taken wildly out of their element to do something new and see what they learned about themselves. We both love Hawaii, and we wanted to bring that love of nature and the ocean and being barefoot on the sand. I wanted to learn to surf. Gary was a surfer.

Before we knew it, we were building the world's most transformational beach party! A modern-day, Gidget-inspired, *Beach Blanket Bingo* teaching leaders to surf in Malibu, California. We decided to call it Into the Fire.

When Gary and I met, we were both in the fire of our lives. Rafe's business was coming together after falling apart, and Gary's wasn't exactly prosperous—plus, he had a baby on the way. There was stress surrounding us, and in the midst of it, we found each other, becoming a calm in each other's storm. We couldn't hide from our lives, we couldn't do things the way we used to do them, so we went straight into the fire, burning through old stories about ourselves, our relationships, even what we believed about life and work. We did life differently. Into the Fire living means accepting and embracing all of life, exactly as it is. You can't go over it, under it, or around it. You must be in it.

My pages of notes, the seeds we planted in the summer of 2012, reflect the core of Into the Fire as it is today: Knowing that experience changes a person. Taking people out of their element. Creating a relaxed, positive, professional, gentle, playful, fun, and optimistic atmosphere. Giving people an opportunity to do a thing they always wanted to do. Drawing in the sand. Making time to connect and be aware of who you are and learning how you impact others when you are relaxed and having a good time and not triggered or under stress. Seeing yourself and being seen. Contrasting stillness with exhilarating challenges. Allowing for failure as an opportunity to learn and grow. Being accepted exactly as you are and growing from there. Celebrating vulnerability. Connecting mindfulness to presence through somatic and embodied awareness exercises. Offering wisdom, unconditional love, and support. And surfing. It was always surfing.

THE SIZE OF MY WORLD

ONE SUMMER DAY, I went into the city to meet Rafe for lunch at his office. It's rare I venture in from our edge of the suburbs.

We moved to the suburbs because we could not afford to buy a home in the city, even as two working professionals. We realized how different the life was here almost immediately—everything is geared toward family life. Parks. Shopping malls. Chain restaurants. Teenagers. We even discussed if we would have chosen to live here if we were not planning to start a family, but soon enough after we had closed escrow, we were expecting Jake.

The contrast of the city to suburb mirrors my former life to my present life.

Though I was dressed in one of my "better" stay-at-home mom outfits, when I compared myself to the women working in the office, I noticed I don't look like them anymore. I had sand in my shoes from a morning at the park with my girl and some colorful stains on my pants from Popsicle drips. In the mom world, I blend in. I drive a big SUV. The backseat is filled with car seats, pretzel crumbs, and Goldfish crackers wedged in unknown places. The trunk is filled with toys and strollers. Not only do I look different, I now live in a world in which I'm prepared for any possible outcome. My priorities have changed. There is no going back.

My world has become smaller. Our lives are more contained now, punctuated by educational television, scheduled naps, and a predictable bedtime routine. One day is not all that different from the next. We do much less, yet our days are more full. At the end of the day when couples without children are out, we are in while our children are asleep, and we catch our breaths to be ready for another day.

My world is smaller so that Jake and Ellie's world can get bigger. Adventures out prepare them for life outside the shelter of our home, and they are exposed to new ideas and experiences. Favorite places see repeat visits so that our children become comfortable in both new and familiar surroundings, and they begin to notice more of the details around them. I can see Jake's understanding of the world growing, too. He can tell me what we will see at certain places, what we did there last time, and maybe what we'll try next time, whether it is at a restaurant, a favorite park, or Disneyland.

I don't think my experience is any different from anyone else who has become a parent. There are two distinct phases of my life—before I had children and after. You can go back to the same places and see the same things, but you certainly don't see with the same eyes.

EXCELLENT ADVENTURES: A CONVERSATION BETWEEN RAFE AND KAREN (CONTINUED)

KAREN: When we were in Hawaii on vacation when Jake was a baby in 2003, it was wild to see how dramatically our life had changed in just two years. We had gone from living in an apartment with both of us working to buying a house, adopting a dog, getting pregnant, me leaving my job, you changing your job, and then having a baby. We needed the break.

RAFE: Wow, when you say it all together, it feels like we weren't doing enough. [*Laughs.*]

KAREN: Then we're there, all relaxed, and I was like, *I don't like our house anymore*. You know, I often say you can't see the picture from inside the frame, and this was one of those moments. Our life had changed, and we were living in a place we bought for "old" us, not "new" us. I had slowly been building up resentments toward the house and how we were living, and I didn't even know it. Our vacation freed me from that.

RAFE: Yeah, that was funny.

KAREN: A change of scenery is good for the soul. You've got to break out of your routine. Try something new.

RAFE: That's a great point. And I guess what I was trying to say when talking about sitting around the campfire is think of something that you would spend money on and do something like that, which will help you figure it out. Like when I went to go ride at that working ranch in Colorado, what you keep calling "cowboy camp," instead of easy and familiar Vegas. I came home a different person. I think that's why certain people may not see the value of coaching because it's not that common to have a coach, but they see the value in having a vacation or a new experience. There are people who come for surfing that don't care about coaching.

KAREN: And I know there are a ton of people who will never get in the ocean because they think it's too scary. You know surfing with us is so incredibly safe.

RAFE: It really is.

KAREN: You almost have a one-on-one lifeguard situation. Nothing bad is going to happen to you.

RAFE: And they are behind you so if you get a shark attack, they are going to eat the lifeguard first.

KAREN: And if there are sharks in Zuma...

RAFE: There are sharks in Zuma.

KAREN: Yeah, there are. But surfing is one of the safest things people can do. Ropes course, one of the safest things people can do with me.

RAFE: Herd immersion?

KAREN: Herd immersion is a little less safe. Race car driving? A little less safe. We make it as safe as we can, but it has to be different to be effective. You can't tune out in the ocean or around horses or driving a race car like you would in a classroom learning about "leadership." The idea of losing control still freaks people out. But the experience changes you, so it's worth taking the risk or at least giving something new a try.

WONDER TWINS

THE DAY AFTER GARY AND I started working on Into the Fire, the Caribou went to another high ropes challenge course. Only here, we had ten minutes to find our partner and create a BRAND NEW experiential workshop. Oh, and we would be leading this about thirty feet up in the trees, and Gary was afraid of heights.

We looked at each other and didn't say much. We had just decided to work together the day before, and we were so awkward in person, and now we had to create ANOTHER original training. Old me would have looked at this situation, saw it going nowhere, and powered through. New me thought *if I've learned anything, I bet we can make this fun together!*

Gary, I have an idea!

I went up to our team leader to ask one key question:

Does it have to be serious?

We led our first ever leadership training on the topic: *How to Choose Shave Ice Like a Local on the North Shore of O'ahu.* Not at all serious, totally life-changing.

After Gary told me he was afraid of heights, I said I'd go up first to help him across the obstacle while he gave the introduction to our workshop. His strength and agility steadied me as we moved together through the challenges, and while we did, we guided our participants on the ground through a visualization of the moments leading up to and including dipping your spoon into the mound of the most refreshing dessert, freshly shaved island snow. As our peers shouted up their favorite flavors and shave ice orders, we completed the workshop, the challenge course, celebrated at the top, and descended as a bonded pair.

After that, we were inseparable...thank goodness because, as we built Into the Fire together, we also pushed each other's buttons and drove each other nuts like siblings do while also doing the most inspired work of our lives.

On off days, Floaty Gary slept through a meeting and Pushy Karen wrote copy solo without consulting her partner, neither of which met our agreements and commitments to each other and the project. We apologized, made it right, talked about what happened, and made stronger agreements. We held ourselves to a higher standard than we ever had, not for ourselves but for each other and for Into the Fire. Most of the days were shining examples of co-creation, so much so that we were a bit embarrassed it was going so well for us when other partnerships in the Caribou were dysfunctional (which we then tried to fix, until the fixing got in the way of our work, and we had to return again to what made us strong).

We believed there was a better way to work and live, so we built it together. It's true. I'm often a salmon swimming upstream. And here I was building a business in partnership with a brand new person. I had to trust the rightness of it and work through the newness of it—being a team (not just a high-performing solo act), having each other's back 100%. Working with Gary was the pinnacle of doing life differently.

When Gary would forget the amazing opportunity to remind people of their vibrancy and aliveness at the beach, wondering who would ever say yes to this radical idea, I'd remind him that I would. When I'd get caught in the details and logistics, getting despondent when the beach house I wanted to rent fell through as we were beginning to invite participants or that the surf instructors I wanted wouldn't call me back, he'd bring me back to the vision we dreamed together and remind me of who we were at our best and told me to drive to the beach to meet with the surf instructors in person and get the deal done. He'd be waiting to hear how it went.

We sanded off each other's rough edges as we clashed and created, and as we did, we became the best of friends. We called ourselves Wonder Twins after Zan and Jayna, the extraterrestrial superheroes we loved from the cartoons we watched as kids growing up in the 1970s in different countries on the same continent. Making Into the Fire happen and doing life differently made us feel like a pair of five-year-old kids playing at the beach. We weren't just working, we were prototyping a new way of life, and we had each other to gently—and not so gently—remind the other of how to be our best.

Gary became one of the most profoundly influential and beloved beings in my life. In the middle of one of my event planning drama queen hysterics, he stopped me, matter of fact, and said, "You're a mess, and I love you anyway. Can we please get back to work?" Creating a vision with a partner to whom I'm not married is a dynamic relationship that continues to grow me.

HELP WANTED

OPTED-OUT, FORMER NONPROFIT EXECUTIVE *seeks extraordinarily flexible part-time employment. Position must be meaningful but not all-consuming with special consideration to causes that stir my heart. Job responsibilities must include only the things I like doing. Salary requirement: make it worth my time. Interested employers may submit a statement of no more than 250 words describing how your position might best suit me. If interested, please call.*

As my children enjoyed summer camp, I started on my own adventure—staging my re-entry into the workforce. It took some getting used to, the idea of transitioning from stay-at-home mom to, hopefully, working-from-home mom. I spent many hours in the past five or so years considering what I'd do next because the work life I'd had in the past was untenable.

Would I return to school for yet another degree?

Try to make ends meet as a never before published freelance writer?

Stuff envelopes?

Send the kids away and work on a fishing boat in Alaska for the summer?

It struck me one day that I didn't have to start over! I'd use my skills to do the things I do best, but I'd do less of them. Once I realized that five years of parenting, watching Oprah, and running a community organization hadn't emptied my brain or professional toolbox, I dusted off my résumé, bought some clothes more appropriate for a boardroom than a playground, and began the hunt.

I was flattered and relieved to receive positive responses to my inquiries and juggled the hiring process with a few potential employers. The first was easy—I sent in a résumé and was called in for an interview. We met, and later the same day they offered me a job. I asked for a few days to consider the offer because, as grateful as I was for the opportunity, I wasn't excited about the work. The next two opportunities seemed even better!

I submitted a writing sample for one and scheduled a second interview with the other. Weeks passed. I was invited for another interview and references were checked. Then the waiting began.

I am confident that if this is indeed the right position, I will get the job. So I'm waiting. And waiting. And waiting. While I am a patient person, waiting for an answer is not one of my strengths.

Waiting makes my mind wander. I amuse myself with the myriad possibilities of how this might all work out well, leading to a dynamic professional life and a paved road ahead of me with all the possibilities lined up as ducks in a row, never having to worry or wonder about work again.

At the same time, I had practically convinced myself that having received no job offer means that I am no longer being considered, and I will be at square one again and that this amazing opportunity that seemed so perfect might have to be put aside for something else, which makes me sad, and I hate that I've invested so much of myself to only start over with the possibility of something else that feels like something *less* because it's not this.

Did I mention waiting is not my strong suit? Patiently (and impatiently), I am holding out hope.

CHOOSING LOVE OVER FEAR

TO OUR SURPRISE AND DELIGHT, the first Into the Fire surf retreat was a resounding success. Our experiment with leadership and surfing—and partnership—worked so well, we agreed to do it again the next summer, and the next, and the next, and the next...with many more to come. (Meanwhile, Circus School remains on the back burner.)

Looking back on who we were when we first met, Gary and I were both simply lost and afraid and didn't know how to say it. Into the Fire got us out of our heads and into our hearts forever.

People come to Into the Fire because they want to believe there is a better way, and they are willing to try surfing because their heart says *yes*. They are lost and afraid, too, and we help them find the way back to themselves, back to the essence and goodness of who they are, just like we did with each other.

Not many adults *think really hard* about surfing and leadership and *decide* it's a good idea. It's crazy! Same with teaching leadership with horses. It doesn't make practical sense. Yet these invitations are beyond a place to learn and grow; we speak to the soul, the spirit of adventure, the desire to believe in what can't be seen. It feels like magic, but it's real, and it boils down to one word: love. Their hearts lead them to us, just like it led me to do this work. Love.

If you have a chance to choose between fear and love, always choose love. It will change your life.

Into the Fire was a miracle. We took a chance to create something bigger than both of us to help people who were like us create, dream, and do differently. We loved the idea of Into the Fire so much we were willing to become the people it needed to make sure it would happen.

Yes, we believed we could do life differently, and now we do.

CON(FIDENCE) WOMAN

"THIS SUIT IS A COSTUME. I am dressed up, but I am no more a working professional than my little girl is actual royalty when dressed in her princess clothes."

These are the stories I tell myself while sitting in the reception area of a high-rise office tower, waiting for my first interview after deciding to go back to work.

I feel like a fraud. A con woman.

To say that I am anxious about my qualifications for employment after devoting five years to professional mothering is one of those ridiculous understatements people make, like saying it's cold out when in the midst of a blizzard. I am a mess of doubt, indecision, and insecurity. I have tangled myself in the belief that my time off has made me irrelevant.

Irrelevant.

Can you imagine?

I feel insignificant.

As though my choice to be at home with my children doesn't matter. As though the work I had done prior, the work I did during, and the work I had the potential to do given my own growth and maturity as a person—now a person who is also a mother—means nothing.

As though I have somehow evaporated into a mist of motherhood.

As if I no longer matter.

I manage to project all the feelings of failure and doubt that I had gathered from taking time away from work and becoming a new mom and transport them five years forward to apply to this new situation where I am so very uncomfortable.

I am irrelevant.

I am also the most important person in the world to two very small humans, critical to the operation of my family unit, integral to the service of mothers in my community, and an essential part of my children's learning and the development of relationships and alliances that will provide the basis of their lifelong education and their abilities to contribute to the world.

On the inside, I am not enough. Being just a mother is not enough. Because I have not been paid for my work, I should not be paid for work and would not be paid for work.

I cannot marginalize or diminish my internal struggle here. Saying it out loud gives me the distance and objectivity to begin exploring something new. I can't see it yet, but I know it is there.

I believe it. I have to. The alternative is so much worse.

I remember the women who commented on my piece about accomplishments. I know I am not the only woman who left her career and had children and then realized I'm not the same person. I can't be the only mom who took a leave, reflected, explored, and wanted work to fit my life and not the other way around. My priorities have changed, I have changed, but now I actually have more to contribute, not less.

I will not give up my time with my kids for my work. I won't sacrifice my work for my life again. The way I've worked feels like it's all or nothing. There's got to be a better way.

#32 ON MY BUCKET LIST: LEARN TO SURF

INTO THE FIRE WAS HAPPENING, but I wasn't planning to surf. I almost let that dream get washed away because of all I thought I was supposed to be.

I wrote my first bucket list when I was twenty-five. Out of college, working full-time, attending graduate school, and single for the first time since I was fifteen, I was free to explore a world of possibilities. The list was practical and aspirational and included things like "learn to make perfect Mexican rice" and "go to Paris."

I was thirty-seven when I updated the list—I'd gone to Paris, mastered the rice, met and married the love of my life, had two happy healthy babies, and was starting to surface as myself again after a period in which I was known to most not as Karen but as Jake and Ellie's Mom. My list of "40 things I want to do before I am 40" was engineered to keep me moving forward and to connect me to who I was becoming, not bound by the history of who I'd been. On that list at #32: learn to surf.

At forty-one, I wrote a new list. Between the first two retreats in the leadership program, I was asked to come up with possibilities of how I might bring my work into the world in a bigger way. This is what I came up with:

- pilot weekly walk & talk women's hiking group

- develop play-based outdoor experiential leadership trainings for high impact leaders, beginning with half-day @ The Reflective Horse (July 2012)

- followed by a half-day ropes course with Fulcrum Adventures (November 2012)

- conduct a workshop on experiential leadership, collaborating with The Reflective Horse (2013)

- develop brand, online strategy, and launch for Excellent Adventures, LLC with simple website and mailing list integration

- cultivate myself as an artist, focusing on developing my skills in photography

- collaborate with Leadership Lab (Carrie Kish) on experiential training for young women leaders

- develop sustainable nonprofit organizational culture project

The first draft of my list was clear, focused, strategic, prioritized, a step in the right direction—and still felt like I was trying to be important and serious all the while creating these amazing, totally excellent adventures. Didn't I know better by now? I edited the list to include:

- pan for gold
- learn to surf (this summer!)
- learn to drive a race car
- dance
- attend professional cooking school
- write a memoir
- pack up the family and move to Paris for three months
- learn to ask for what I want and how to use this to serve others
- plan family trips to Italy and Israel

Surfing had been on my bucket list for YEARS, and as we created Into the Fire, I could almost feel the wax beneath my feet…and then I decided it wasn't the right time for me. In my mind, we specifically designed the retreat for EVERYONE ELSE to have an incredible once-in-a-lifetime, bucket-list worthy experience—but not me. I was the co-leader. I had a job to do.

It was a deeply ingrained, learned behavior to always consider the needs of others before my own. Yet the essence of Into the Fire is the belief we could do differently, so how could I in good conscience do the same old thing? It occurred to me that this retreat might also be a place for *me* to learn and grow as a leader and also have the time of my life.

Doing differently also meant talking about my dilemma with Rafe and Gary and saying out loud what I wanted, what I needed, and what I worried about instead of keeping it to myself and cycling the thoughts in my head. Doing differently meant listening to and trusting when EVERYONE I ASKED TOLD ME I should surf. Doing differently meant leading while learning at the same time as the people we were teaching. We were not going to be the ultimate experts I assumed leaders were supposed to be.

On top of all that, when and *if* I surfed, I would then be co-leading the second half of the retreat with wet hair and no makeup. *So unprofessional,* said the old part of me who kept forgetting about doing differently while imagining hiding in the public restroom at Zuma Beach with a blow dryer *if there were even functioning electrical outlets*. There ABSOLUTELY had to be a better way—and I was determined to do it!

I thought leadership had to be stiff and formal, but I learned through experience that my authentic leadership starts with courage, commitment, self-awareness, and a sense of humor. It's risky and vulnerable and proven to be the best way to create a deep and real connection.

Just like everyone else, I struggled to get into a wetsuit and worried about what might be swimming beneath me. I surfed. I fell off my board a lot. I had one of the best days of my life.

The very same day I learned to surf, I also became a person who teaches leadership through surfing. I'd never done that before, and then I did. I was beginning to see myself in a whole new way, and as soon as I did, as if out of nowhere, the opportunities in front of me became far more interesting and exciting. This was *my* better way.

WHEN ONE DOOR CLOSES...

I'VE NOW BEEN THROUGH FOUR interview processes, have yielded two job offers, and am still unemployed. Despite this, I feel great about starting over, even though the last job offer felt like a personal challenge where I had to determine just how much I'm willing to compromise. Do I really want this, or do I want to take a bigger risk and work on my own terms?

I had to pass. As that door closed, another opened quickly. I began asking anyone I knew if they knew people who needed what I do and someone did! Two days after I turned down what I thought to be the perfect job, I interviewed for an EVEN MORE perfect job! Sure there were a couple of concerns, but this job really was going to be PERFECT!

Almost as swiftly as the new door opened, I turn around, and it hits me squarely on my ass.

As the phone rings, I anticipate good news. How could it be anything but? And then, I hear her voice. The sound of consolation. I am being handled.

"First, I want to tell you how much I enjoyed meeting you."

Crap, it's over. The perfect job with its convenient location, impossibly ideal hours, the pinnacle of my education and expertise, was going to someone else. I set down the phone, and for the first time in my job search process, I cry.

This kind of rejection is new for me, the overachieving perfectionist that I am. Rarely, if ever, do I invest myself so fully in a process not to reach my desired or intended outcome. I'm good at reading situations, am very intuitive as information is presented, and generally have a sense of if something will work for me or not.

Even though I had a few concerns, I am stunned. I feel lost.

When I set out on this quest for part-time employment, I had a solid idea of what work I could do, work that would work for me. Now, I'm not so sure.

I'm reminded of this scene from *Say Anything* where the hero, Lloyd Dobler, defines his future career path:

> *I don't want to sell anything, buy anything, or process anything as a career. I don't want to sell anything bought or processed, or buy anything sold or processed, or process anything sold, bought, or processed, or repair anything sold, bought, or processed. You know, as a career, I don't want to do that.*

There is a whole lot that I don't want to do, like start a job that cannot be done or work for someone who tells me one thing one day and its opposite the next. I don't want to commute for several hours a day, nor am I interested in sacrificing my time with my children to barely cover the costs of their care.

I don't want to start over, and I don't want to do what I did before.

I don't know what to do.

STAY STOKED

WHAT WAS I THINKING? Not only did I want to learn to surf but now potentially base my livelihood on it?

When Gary and I started Into the Fire, I found the stoke.

Surfers use the word stoke as an adjective: to be "stoked" is to be completely and intensely enthusiastic, exhilarated, or excited about something. When you are stoked, there is no limit to what you can do. As a verb, its definitions include tending to or adding fuel to a fire and increasing the amount of strength to something.

I surfed once at our first retreat in 2012 and again at our retreat in 2013, testing it out to see if the stoke was a fluke. It wasn't. I wanted more. The following year, I took a solo lesson. I needed to give myself what we had been giving others. It worked for them, maybe it would work for me.

During the lesson, I observed my mental conversations like I would in meditation. I noticed that it takes me a while to get out of my head and be where I am in the moment, even when I've paid for a private surf lesson. Pretty stubborn, Gidge.

In the water with my instructor and my board, I was thinking about how I'd tell Rafe and the kids about it, what I could use about it for an article I was writing, how I could translate the experience for my clients—all this while also trying to pop up, catch, and ride a wave!

Then, I was surfing. I. Was. SURFING. It felt like magic. Time stopped, and all I knew was me in the ocean. No outside pressure to perform, no inner judgment, no expectation of how I was supposed to be. Nothing existed outside of my being in that single, solitary moment, and that moment was perfect. Zen, bliss, heaven, oneness—words attempting to describe the indescribable connection between the Universe and me when I was surfing.

Like Clark Kent becoming Superman in a phone booth, Wonder Woman spinning to emerge clad in indestructible bracelets paired with her Lasso of Truth, I was and am transformed. In the ocean, I am powerful in ways I'm not on land. Zipped into a wetsuit with a board under my arm, I have powers that I've never known anywhere else. I am Surfer Girl.

Surfing has offered me infinite opportunities to stay present in the moment—a challenge for a habitual future-seeker with big plans. My time in the water has given me a depth of presence and ability to stay with life as it is and not how I might want it to be. In the ocean, you don't know what the next wave will bring, and it really doesn't matter what's next if you're not aware of where you are right now.

Surfing has also given me the confidence—and humility—to try other new sports. To improve my paddling, I've enrolled in swim lessons in the lane next to Ellie. Every day, I'm reminded of the joy of being a beginner, which was lost during the years I was busy being great at my job but not so great at being Karen.

My work is now an extension of my life and not the other way around. Pursuing surfing makes me happy. I have to make the time to take care of my whole self—which means sticking to the hours I've scheduled to work with clients and ending my days so I can be at the beach and training to be in the water.

Like leadership, surfing is something you have to feel, not just think about, to do well.

I have found that when feeling burned out, it's important to take a break from the action and go to the people, places, and things that inspire you. When you do, you fuel yourself.

My inner wisdom gently guides me: *Find what lights your fire, do whatever it takes to stoke yourself, and, by all means, stay stoked.*

THE LIST, PART 2

I AM HEARTBROKEN BY POTENTIAL EMPLOYERS.

I decide I'll write a new List, like the one I wrote before I met Rafe. This time, I want to find my career soulmate. I have moped and obsessed about the jobs I declined, the ones that rejected me, and am being reminded how often and quickly I am willing to overlook the red flags when I hope something is a right fit. I can be more disciplined moving forward. It worked before for something far more important, why not do it again?

I went from looking for the right job to looking for any job where I could earn a modest living and do something new that I might not have otherwise considered. Egg donor or surrogate? No, I'm probably too old. Nitpicker? Why, yes, I am detail oriented, but no, I don't want to comb hair for lice. I'd hate to bring my work home with me.

With a little help from Google, P.I., I decide against applying to work with the guy who's turned over a new leaf after being indicted or the woman who is in ongoing litigation with an allegedly cult-like religious group. It might be hard to find the right thing, but it would be even harder to do something wrong.

The voice inside me says *don't settle when you want to follow your heart*.

Much like the love of my life, I am insistent that my job meets my requirements. I start thinking about the New List to define my career objectives to find work that is:

- challenging but not impossible.

- involved creatively in problem solving but not problems that are only solved directly or indirectly with fundraising.

- flexible and/or part-time, starting at about twenty hours a week with the potential to evolve into something flexible/full-time in the next three years.

- related to a cause I find meaningful and relevant.

- local, does not involve a lengthy commute or extensive obligations to travel.

- able to compensate me at a rate that is commensurate with my work experience.

- personally engaging, allowing me to collaborate with other professionals.

Not quite 100 qualifications—perhaps I've become a bit more open-minded and flexible over time. And I only need one person to hire me. One.

With the rough draft of the New List in my hand, I receive a call from an old boss who asks me to work with him on a project for the next few months.

A few months is something. I'll be working. I can do this as long as I don't lose myself in the process and end up heartbroken again.

GOOD LUCK, GIDGET.

"ONE DAY, THAT WILL BE ME."

It was a cool spring morning when I decided to go for a run at Zuma Beach. I saw a woman walking out of the water carrying her board with a grace and confidence so powerful. I saw her and wanted to BE her.

I said it with such certainty, such conviction and determination, even I believed myself...right until that familiar comforting/condescending little voice inside my head started chattering, "Honey, that girl is an athlete in her twenties and probably learned to surf before she could walk. Good luck, Gidget."

What was I thinking?

Learning to surf as a wannabe athletic forty-four-year-old suburban wife and mother of two doesn't make logical, rational sense. The more I thought about it, it actually seemed like a terrible idea. I've got an inventory of injuries from a life well lived, I'm not a great swimmer, and I don't really like being wet.

Yet somehow in that surfer girl, I saw myself.

I wasn't born with it, even though I was born in Huntington Beach, home of the Vans US Open of Surfing, and spent my teenage years on the dry and sandy parts of Salt Creek, T Street, and Trestles—world-renowned surf breaks. Surfing was all around me, but it certainly wasn't *me*. I was the girl who sat on the honor roll and student government, volunteered, and saw a hard and straight path to a magnificent future. I saw the surfer lifestyle—drugs, bleached blonde hair, and a bunch of burnouts with a "who cares" attitude—as a one-way ticket to nowhere. Of course, I watched reruns of the vintage Gidget TV show from the 60s and imagined my life hanging in the waves with Moondoggie and Kahuna, but it was an indulgence, like eating an entire sleeve of Oreos dipped in whole milk. Fun, but not something you'd actually do if you were trying to get somewhere.

Nearly twenty-five years later, I find myself at a crossroads. Exhausted. I'd driven myself so fast I literally crashed. After recovering and starting a new career as a life coach and thinking I was getting good at this whole "comfortable with not knowing and trusting myself" routine, I still wasn't content. I was still striving, and it got me exactly nowhere, and even though I feared my life was as good as it would get, inside me there was a spark that told me there was something more.

Who was the burnout now?

Just like when I started coaching, I knew I couldn't be the only one who felt like this. I knew too many people like me who wanted out. We had to get out of the grind, had to break the cycle and unrelenting quest of finding the mythical unicorn of work/life balance. It didn't exist.

There had to be a better way.

Management guru Peter Drucker is credited with saying, "The best way to predict the future is to create it." In that moment, I realized I was imagining a future for myself that would likely be as stressful and empty as my past, I knew I had to change it, so I listened to my Gidget-watching, Oreo-eating wild heart and mentally recommitted to checking surfing off my bucket list for real this time, along with driving a race car and learning to fly on a trapeze.

LOWENSTEIN

I AM NOW A WORKING MOTHER. I know how to get a job and work. I know how to parent. Combining the two is a mystery.

Work-life balance? Ha! I struggled for MONTHS tottering along the edge of working and not. As hard as it once was to imagine life with a child, it is now impossible to picture life with children AND work. Being a full-time stay-at-home parent is a lot to manage, but it's not even in the same neighborhood of trying to manage the demands of a family along with the needs of an employer. It's like comparing apples to alligators.

"How will it look?" I asked anyone who would listen. *How would I keep all the balls in the air? Would they keep hitting me in the head and bouncing off each other? Would I work part-time? Full-time? On site? From home? Commute? Local? How would the children manage? Would I be able to be an active parent volunteer? Would I get to know the families in each child's class? Would I miss out on all the chats and coffees of the stay-at-home moms who had their kids on a shorter schedule? Would it matter? Would I have time for myself? The gym? Keeping house? Would it be enough? Would a part-time salary, offset by the added expenses of daycare, make a difference? Would I be enough? Had my break made my job skills irrelevant? Could I do part-time work and still make a meaningful contribution? Would I feel good about doing less?*

It's been a week, and I am filled with mixed emotions. I am relieved, grateful, and happy to be working. Yet every day for the first week, I cried. Frustrated, bored, guilty, and exhausted.

I know the truth: I missed it. I missed feeling valued and productive in a way that being a stay-at-home mother had not fulfilled me. But I also mourn. I mourn for the loss of my freedom. I mourn having Ellie in daycare after preschool because with Jake, I was always home. My days are a race against the clock: up before 6:00, everyone downstairs and dressed by 6:45, out the door at 7:15. Drop Jake at kindergarten. Drop Ellie at preschool. Sit in traffic. Work. Race back for Ellie. Run errands. Pick up Jake. Think about dinner, going to the gym, and doing any and all that I'm not able to do that I didn't question a week before. This is what people have been doing all the time. This is what I do now. And while it's what I do, it's not who I am.

By the end of the week, I began to accept my new circumstances. I need to work. I want to work. I am working. I now relate differently to the other mothers, the working ones, as a new initiate into an established sisterhood. Its doctrines include: 1) yes, it is hard, and 2) you do what you have to do.

As a new member of this sisterhood, I'm learning a few things.

I can be good at being both a mom and an employee. The two are not mutually exclusive. To do both, I have to juggle with great agility, organization, and determination. I am now critically aware of how I spend my minutes, regardless of whether or not I am paid for them.

I know now that no matter how Ellie protests about her extended days at school, she adapts.

I know that, no matter how tired I am at the end of the day, if I don't pack up lunches and backpacks for everyone the night before, the morning rush is terribly unpleasant.

I know that with their teachers and grandparents, my children are in great care whether they are with me or not.

I know that I can do this now.

Now, at the end of each working day, I am grateful. I'm not angry or sad, thinking about the drive, the struggle, the juggle, or the sacrifice. I think about why I am working, why I do anything at all.

I do this for my family. I do this for myself. I do this because I must. I do it for love. Rafe, Jake, Ellie.

I am reminded of the closing words in *The Prince of Tides*:

> *At the end of every day, I drive through the city of Charleston, and I cross the bridge that will take me home. I feel the words building inside me, I can't stop them or tell you why I say them, but as I reach the top of the bridge, these words come to me in a whisper. I say these words as a prayer, as regret, as praise, I say: Lowenstein, Lowenstein.*

Rafe. Jake. Ellie. Home. Family.

Love.

It's why I do what I do.

THE SPIRITUAL MECHANIC

I WAS WORKING OFF OF AN OUTDATED operating system where I could only realize something had to change when I had absolutely nothing left to give.

In 2015, I had an injury from horseback riding that had me stop exercising, then I had surgery on a different body part and six weeks of recovery, which led me directly into a trip to Costa Rica to support a client piloting her own surf leadership program. Whew! I came home from Costa Rica and the next day met up with Gary to dive into finalizing our first weekend-long Into the Fire, scheduled for a few weeks later.

This retreat felt like we were creating a brand new business. Here I was in the midst of getting ready to do this thing we'd never done, largely with people we didn't know, and with the stakes so much higher than before. Gary and I were sitting on the floor of my office working on timelines when Rafe came in and said his dad—Papi to all of us—was being hospitalized, but no one knew what was wrong. We had to consider the very real possibility that I might not be leading this very big deal retreat that had people flying in from all over if my father-in-law didn't make it. It was intense to say the least.

Rafe's dad came home from the hospital, undiagnosed but stable as we opened our fourth Into the Fire. Three days after the retreat ended, my kids' school year ended, and we went up to the ranch to drop off our dogs before leaving on vacation to Hawaii. Before we even left for the trip, Jake's horse Fluttershy needed emergency surgery and ended up in the ICU. If we hadn't caught her in distress, we probably would have lost her in the night. With two days before we're scheduled to leave for vacation, we didn't know if we'd have to cancel if Papi took a turn for the worse.

He didn't, and all was well enough, so we left. I surfed in Hawaii for the first time and overused my weak shoulder because surfing was so awesome, and I'd forgotten that I was out of shape. Then I couldn't drive. Instead of relaxing, I sat on the lanai researching physical therapists to see when I got home.

Monday after we landed, I drove the 100 miles up to our ranch to pick up our dogs and play hostess to Gary's mom and aunt, who were visiting Santa Barbara (and whom I simply adore) after Gary had told them about our ranch. I picked them up and drove them out to our quaint rural town and acres of horses in wine country. In the midst of shopping and lunch and with miles to go in my day, I received a text from Rafe telling me Papi had started chemo. When we left on vacation merely days before, we didn't know he had cancer.

I was back to work on Tuesday. On Thursday, I had to release a client from coaching because she had fallen into a severe depression and needed to be working with her therapist, not me.

I hung up the phone and started crying.

I couldn't stop.

Rafe came home hours later to find me in bed sobbing. He listened while I tried to piece together what happened that broke me. Rafe consults, and as he heard my words, he kindly offered that with his clients, he never takes on their problems as his own. As he said that, my face lit up. I had no idea how many problems and emotions I'd taken on as my own. Everyone's shit was now my shit. No wonder I couldn't handle one more thing.

I asked coaches I knew for specific help to fix my mojo. I wanted a spiritual mechanic and found Megan. Here's what I wrote to her:

It's not a usual pattern for me to take on energy—I typically keep my side of the fence clean (or so I like to think). This week, I got pummeled, and I didn't even see it coming. I thought I might be in the midst of a panic attack (which I've never had, but I felt pretty awful).

Megan gave me detailed homework to help me nurture myself. Gary insisted I stop taking care of everyone else and instructed me to take a three-month sabbatical. I completed engagements with several clients and took on the least amount of work I could to stay connected and be able to restore my energy.

In hindsight, even though I had really good boundaries, I couldn't see how hard I'd been pushing (again) and how much everyone and everything else was affecting me. It's amazing how many times I had to keep learning the same lessons to go deeper into understanding myself.

As Papi's health declined, I was able to rebuild my reserves to be there for Rafe and his family while taking care of ours and myself because, in the midst of all this, we were also counting down the days to Jake's Bar Mitzvah. In the last family moment we shared with my father-in-law before he passed, we laughed together and celebrated life, all of it.

DYING INSIDE?

COACHING IS NOT EASY TO EXPLAIN but is very easy to experience. I could tell you what it feels like to walk from the sand into the ocean in Hawaii. I could describe lazy glances of the island map while eating fresh, ripe tropical fruit for breakfast and deciding where to discover the perfect beach. I could tell you how I long for the warm water when I'm in California and how I rush into the ocean, squishing the sand between my toes, sand so soft you could practically bake a cake with it. I could tell you about the little gasp of air and hesitation before the tide rushes forward and the moment I relax into its warm ebb and gentle flow.

I could tell you all of this, but your experience of Hawaii and mine might be completely different, and the only way to really know how it feels is to feel it for yourself. The feeling, not the description, stays in your memory.

Coaches dwell in the land of imagination, possibility, vision, and creativity...sometimes. Other times, it's entirely objective. Coaches point out things that may not be obvious to you...or things that are. They dig deep. They celebrate. They challenge and support. They want you to have what you want.

The first time I hired a coach, I did so because someone told me it would be good for me. I knew the value of coaching from my training. I had Big Ideas, perhaps too big, or at least big enough that I've found myself crushed under the weight of expectations I've piled on top of myself—for a while, I've wanted to be the WORLD'S LEADING EXPERT on mothers returning to work.

In addition to this crushing goal I'm not sure matters to me anymore, I notice there are other areas of my life where I've stopped thriving and started just showing up.

How could I be miserable? I am a working mom and budding entrepreneur building my coaching business after hours and have the best job I could imagine at this time. It is close to home, flexible, close to the kids, so many great things about it. As I am speaking to a coach about it, out came these words: **Every day I go to work, a tiny part of me is dying inside.**

Did I just say that OUT LOUD?!

DYING INSIDE: A CONVERSATION BETWEEN RAFE AND KAREN

RAFE: If you are dying a little inside every day, the hell with that. That sucks. Do anything else. Anything.

KAREN: I was really surprised. It was really hard for me to admit it.

RAFE: Why? You said it so many times to me. It was like, "Hi, I'm Karen, I'm dying inside." That was you. That was not hard at all.

KAREN: No, but to say it, write it, and publish it. To send that out to people I knew and put on my website in a blog post. I never wanted to seem like I was ungrateful for my job. Seriously.

RAFE: That's fair.

KAREN: And I hated that I was saying that because I had practically invented that job for myself.

RAFE: Yeah, you could have done a better job with that. Made it a little better. "I'm going to create this job, but I'm not going to like it because I'm dying a little bit every day when I'm here." That was a terrible job. I couldn't wait to tell you to leave.

KAREN: You did. All the time. But I had already started down a path I was working on, and I wasn't ready to leave. I really didn't want to sound ungrateful.

RAFE: You weren't ungrateful. It just wasn't for you.

KAREN: I didn't want people to feel like I didn't want to work hard.

RAFE: Like honestly, who cares! If you are actually dying a little inside, you owe it to yourself more than the people around you to do something about it.

KAREN: Yeah. I didn't see an out, though.

RAFE: It wasn't hard for me to say that my business was killing me and that I hated it even though it was the best of all things.

KAREN: Even though it was hard for me to say, it's probably the most resonant thing I've shared. I've had so many people get in touch with me about it like, hey, that thing you said about dying inside, I feel like that, too. It's devastating and so liberating to say out loud. Once you say it, you can do something about it.

TRAUMA BRAIN, PART 2

I DIDN'T KNOW I WAS experiencing anxiety until the therapist asked me what was happening when I couldn't stop crying and felt like I couldn't breathe. My breath was shallow. My ears were ringing. My heart was beating fast. My hands were sweating. He told me I was flooded with emotions, and we needed to stop because I could no longer process the feelings or the experience. That was new. After that, I started noticing what triggered the feelings of anxiety and wrote them down instead of ignoring them and pushing through.

I messaged Gary after every therapy session.

> **KAREN**: After I saw you in Hawaii, something happened in a conversation I was having with Rafe and Emma. We were talking about how the past affects us, choices we make, etc., and it occurred to me how often (daily, a lot), I throw myself into past memories of things gone wrong. A lot of the stuff I've been listening to/reading around somatic work, sensitivity, led me to see that maybe there's something I am ready to see differently now. I found a therapist with a practice in somatic experiencing—among other modalities—to talk about it. What I didn't know, couldn't see honestly and truly, was how often I get flooded with anxiety and emotional overwhelm. It was

crazy and awesome and unfamiliar to connect the feeling in my body with the awareness of shortness of breath, heart palpitations, ringing in my ears, spaced out tunnel vision—I never noticed how I react to a bunch of stuff, but now I am. I now have a running list of what happens right before I start getting the pain in my chest, like getting texts or getting startled by a noise, or whatever else...Sharing because this is new. Sharing because it feels like I'm out there in the trees 30 feet above the ground and I know you have my back 100%-100%. I know I'm safe. I know it is the right time to work on this. I know I will be ok. I'm also scared, and that's ok too. The doctor is as ancient as the trees, kind and gentle. I go on Fridays.

KAREN: I learned something about myself that might be useful for your clients. Apparently, what feels very slow to me is epic growth. My tendency is to minimize my progress in the quest for what's next, judging my actions instead of reflecting. Ouch.

KAREN: Sitting in my car after session with the doctor. We started digging into my childhood trauma today. Connected a feeling to the experience I didn't know I had: shame. Not around my dad dying but not being good enough for my mom to love or nurture. It's heavy and light at the same time. I'm glad I'm here.

GARY: Freedom is right here...sending love my dear ITF partner—quick question what do you think causes that feeling?

KAREN: Attachment to a very very old comfortable ugly sweater of a story and all the behaviors I created to support the belief, never questioning it, I believed it so hard, I feel like a tumor has been removed. I'm in shock.

KAREN: What's new today—speaking out loud to Rafe feelings and experiences that up until now have been easier to keep hidden. Allowing a flood of love and compassion toward myself as I presence and heal these traumas. Allowing for the process to unfold, to be exactly where I am, knowing and trusting that I am here at exactly the right time. Keeping the focus on me, not looking for how to teach or share my process. Thank you for holding and staying. Thanks to me, too, for doing the work.

KAREN: Today in therapy: getting in touch with anger and power, learning to allow for simplicity when my mind tends toward complexity, finding the space for me to be me and not try to fit into a mold of how I think I need to be to shrink into others' concept of me and what works for them. Or like I said, making complex simpler.

KAREN: Dude, I'm so glad I chose this. It's the ultimate Into the Fire.

KAREN: I have fought with reality so hard for so long, it will be a new world—truly—to be at peace with what is. I'm

> beginning. It's new. To actually feel feelings, not just the ones I prefer. To actually be here.

> **GARY**: Finally.

> **KAREN**: I have now graduated from therapy. I am a miracle! Past is behind me and always a part of me.

I didn't know how to feel anger. I spent years burying my emotions as deeply as I could to not have to experience the pain and the truth: what happened in my childhood was tragic and sad. Not only that, it was over…everywhere but in my mind, where I've kept trying to rebuild the house from ashes.

Instead of anger, I felt frustrated. I turned the anger toward myself, until one day I realized that anger is a "normal" feeling and doesn't have to be expressed or directed as uncontrollable rage. Anger can be assertive and active. Because I was willing to look at it, I had the power to change it, no matter how long it would take me to get there.

BORN TO LOVE

I REALLY DIDN'T WANT A PUPPY. Our kids were just old enough to not feel like babies anymore when we returned from a trip to Europe with our six- and eight-year-old adventurers. With the end of naps and the beginning of both kids in the same school at the same time, our life was starting to be easy, and A PUPPY IS NOT EASY.

The responsibilities? The training? You've got to be kidding me.

Wait, what? There is a litter of rescued purebred Doberman puppies, and they think they have a match for our family? Let's go get the kids and see!

Indy. Indiana Jones Pery. Our Indian Red.

I didn't know Indy was going to be my dog. He was supposed to be Rafe's fortieth birthday dog and a companion for Daisy, who now eleven (a sage senior citizen in dog years) needed something new to drag her tired old bones off the couch.

One day when Rafe was bringing Indy inside after a quick trip to the lawn, our little guy ran straight for me like I was the only thing in the world that mattered to him. Such love! Such loyalty! I'd always been around dogs, but I never had one of *those* dogs. The way he looked at me, he stole my heart.

Oh, how I loved that dog, and I loved being loved by that dog... even when he sent me to the emergency room with what I thought was a concussion.

I loved him when he sent me back to the ER with a broken nose, which happened as he ran full speed to cuddle with me on the bed and knocked into my face.

I loved him so much. We were inseparable. We were each other's pillow.

I said so many times out loud how I believed Indy was put on this planet to love me. I love my people, and my people love me, but no one loved me the way Indy did.

I loved him for how much he loved Daisy as she slowed down and couldn't play anymore and how much he respected her canine authority until her very last day on Earth. I loved him for how quickly he and Ruby bonded at the Doberman rescue when it was time to welcome a new member to our family. I loved him for how much he loved.

I loved him when we spent his first birthday at the ER after he'd stolen two pounds of grapes off the counter—and I hold a very special place in my heart for the vet tech who counted the two pounds of grapes after they'd induced vomiting to make sure he wasn't poisoned from eating them.

I loved him when we spent his fifth birthday back in the ER when his gums had suddenly turned from pink to grey and his mouth was cold. The cough we hoped to cure with antibiotics was actually pneumonia, a complication of a genetic condition—dilated cardiomyopathy (DCM), which affects an unfortunate number of purebred Dobies—and his heart was failing.

How could it be true?

He never stopped being his exuberant self, never slowed down, never told us that our days together were coming to an end.

I loved him when the doctor said he might have a few weeks, maybe months to live.

I loved him when our eyes met in the veterinary hospital where he received oxygen, and I told him what a good boy he was. I loved him when I gave consent for the vet to give him CPR if his heart stopped while they were monitoring him overnight to see if he would stabilize and we could bring him home.

He never came home.

Our sweet puppy left us a few hours after we said goodnight. The shock took me back to the moment I learned my Daddy had died, but now I cried oceans of tears for the loves I had lost. It is unfathomable to feel so much love and pain in the same heartbeat. It is impossible to believe you will ever love again, to ever be so vulnerable knowing that you can and will be broken hearted again. Yet we do. To love is to live, and love is eternal.

Indy, our dog whose job on Earth was to love, died because his heart was too big.

WAVES BREAK

And it is exceedingly short, his galloping life. Dog's die so soon. I have my stories of that grief, no doubt many of you do also. It is almost a failure of will, a failure of love, to let them grow old—or so it feels. We would do anything to keep them with us and to keep them young. The one gift we cannot give. – Mary Oliver, *Dog Songs*

I MISS MY INDY SO MUCH.

He was here, and now he's not. I know that life is impermanent, but today it's hitting me pretty hard.

There are moments of days when I am fine, sometimes even fabulous, and then I'm not. Now I'm not. I will be again. Waves break.

When people ask, "Is there anything I can do," I ask if they could bring him back—not in a Stephen King *Pet Sematary* sort of way. I don't think I'd like that at all.

Today, I'm struck by all the experiences we'll never have again. I'll never see him stretch when he comes out of his crate in the morning nor the circles he'd spin in the carpet as if rubbing the sleep from his eyes.

I know it's temporary.

I found an article about the stages of grief that reminded me of what I had read all those years ago after the crash of 2002. Like the rest of life, grief is not a linear progression with mile markers that tell you how far you've gone. It's more like waves—back and forth and under and through.

I went to surf at Zuma on Monday morning after what was probably seven months of not surfing. It was not an easy day to surf. El Niño storms had shaken up our waters, and the waves were fast, hard, and unrelenting. I spent the first part of my session with my instructor swimming against the current and getting nowhere.

We went back to shore for a quick debrief. I was stuck in a current I couldn't see from the sand. No wonder I couldn't paddle past it.

Learning to surf, before we go into the water, we watch the waves to see what they tell us. We look for patterns in what we observe—wind, currents, how are the waves breaking, right or left, fast or slow. We do this longer than I'd think necessary. Once you get in the ocean, you are part of the story as it unfolds, wherever it takes you.

I think the most frustrating days of surfing are when you fight the conditions. If it's flat, it's flat, and you're probably not going to catch much—if anything. You have to be with the ocean exactly as it is—it doesn't have an agenda, and whatever the waves give you, it's certainly not personal.

The worst place to be in the ocean is right where the waves are breaking. We think we want to go above them so we can see, maybe feel like we've got some bit of control, but it's actually easier to go under and wait until they pass or paddle out just beyond the break.

To surf, you have to catch the wave before it breaks, to meet its energy with yours—that's what moves you forward. You're with it—not under it, in front of it, or behind it. You have to be with the wave to ride it.

I think this is how grief moves, too.

I'd forgotten the connection until the ocean reminded me of where I still had work to do—both to grieve and to get stronger.

I don't love swimming, but I love surfing, so I have to paddle. You do what you have to do to be who you need to be to live the life you love. It's hardly ever glamorous, whether it's sweating through hours of yoga, baring your soul to your coach or therapist, sitting alone with feelings you've never felt, swimming infinite laps in the pool, or finding a way to say goodbye.

Some heartbreaks never heal and instead they leave us open; not scarred but more tender, raw, and real. I was shattered when I lost my Indy, and I know loving him and being loved by him grew my capacity to love exponentially. I think since losing him I've become more like him—more lovable, more giving, more open and accepting.

WAKE-UP WEDNESDAY

WEDNESDAY, JANUARY 9, 2013, is the next in a series of experiential networking meetups I'm hosting. First was networking and miniature golf, next was bowling, now ice skating.

Drops of blood splash on the crisp, white ice of the skating rink. A team of paramedics rolls in a stretcher. Everything stops. Hushed voices. "Is she okay?" Against medical advice, the paramedics release her to my care, and I drive to the emergency room. "This is going to hurt," they say as they numb her scalp before stapling closed the laceration on the back of her head. I hold her hands, we both look down. We wait for a CT Scan. Waiting. Waiting.

It was *not* supposed to be like this.

I close my eyes, and I see it again. My dear friend Beth is skating like an Olympian on the ice, then her skates slip from beneath her feet as if a rug had been pulled out from beneath her. It happens too quickly, there is no time for her to catch herself. She falls straight back like a tree falling in the forest, and *everyone* hears. We all stop, stunned, both by the sound of it and by the bright red spots of blood spattered onto the stark blue white surface of the skating rink. The paramedics arrive. We drive to the emergency room. I hold her hands as they staple her back together. Three staples in her head. Blood is dried onto the back of her neck. Waiting. Waiting. She is scared. I am scared. We both attempt calm and collected. We are, and we are not.

She calls me later. "What did they say to do if the bleeding doesn't stop?" I can't remember, I don't think they told us.

This wasn't how the day was supposed to go. Not at all.

Here's how else the day went: we had a great time together. We laughed. We shared stories. We supported each other. The friends who'd been skating with us that day all reached out like neighbors in a community—how can we help? When can we do this again? She was in good hands with every caregiver (especially the team of strong and able paramedics who tended to her like knights to a lady-in-waiting), and I wouldn't have done a thing differently. As she canceled her plans for the evening with good humor, she reminded me of something I often say: it's either a good experience or a good story. This was neither and both.

Weeks later, she tells me it was a turning point for her, a huge wake-up call that Wednesday. Looking back, she says, it sounds like a much bigger deal than it was. Things happen. We can't let our fears and anxiety get in the way of living.

Am I going to do things differently? Of course. A part of me is scared, scared that the next adventure I lead will end with worse results than a fall on the ice or a surfboard bonk on the head. That part of me would rather hide safely in my office, coming up with great ideas that never get executed, fear operating as my CEO.

The rest of me says *holy shit!* What happened that day was a breakthrough, and I got to be a part of something truly amazing. I see it every time. When people step outside their comfort zones and take risks, when they can see themselves differently, lives change. Doors open. Magic happens.

Of course I'm scared, but I've yet to see a fairy-tale happy ending without facing a dragon.

NO REQUESTS ARE OFF LIMITS

EMMA WAS THE FIRST PARTICIPANT to say yes to the Fifth Annual Into the Fire Surf Retreat.

A few weeks before the retreat, we sent questions to all of our participants, including this:

Do you have any requests that will make Into the Fire the best weekend of your life? No requests are off limits. We create Into the Fire with you and for you. Let us delight you!

Emma responded but made no requests. But because we'd been connecting all summer and knew why she was coming and what she wanted for herself, we wrote back: *Are you up for a challenge? This question is not intended simply to gather information to keep you safe, happy, and healthy; this is an invitation for you to ask for ANYTHING—not just for ITF but also for life, for the future you are creating. Dream, play, give us a challenge. Be indulgent, specific, and have fun with it!*

Gary and I encouraged her to be open, both to ask and be willing to receive. She took a few days and sent us back a detailed list. Among her requests...

Surf an inflatable unicorn! LOL! I had to put that in there.

Her request spoke to my heart. Through the years of creating each Into the Fire retreat, we experimented with details that added a personal touch and our signature stamp of love, from adding shade tents and sand toys to baking cookies for our guests that Kanako made for me when I visited Vancouver. Knowing both how important it is to ask for what you want and how hard it can be to do so, it was important to us that we gave Emma and the other retreat participants permission to make requests to add to their overall retreat experience. I didn't tell Gary that we needed to work a giant inflatable unicorn into our agenda until he arrived in Los Angeles a few days before the retreat.

In the "Book of Leadership According to Karen Pery," one of the guiding principles of developing leaders is: **you have to be yourself**.

Imagine a great team. For you it might be sports, for me it's a restaurant. Everyone has to know their job, be committed to a shared vision of success, own their strengths, and perform their role to the best of their abilities while communicating with others and paying attention to what's happening around them for the team to succeed. The chef gets the best from her suppliers to create her menu, the host keeps the reservations moving, the wait staff delivers orders to the kitchen and takes care of customers' allergies and celebrations, the dishwashers keep the supplies in check, and every cook runs their station from salads to desserts. At the end of the night, you have happy, loyal customers who've had a great experience and look forward to another, everyone gets paid, and the restaurant continues to serve.

Everyone has to do his or her part.

I believe that leadership is synonymous with self-awareness. You need to be you and I need to be me so fully and authentically that there are no questions or doubts. The better I know me, the more I am able to see you. I am confident and secure. When I am full and include you in my world, you get to be you fully. There's room for all of us to grow. If I'm constantly shifting who I think I'm supposed to be, I am a shadow of myself, more outside than inside. You may find what you need, but I am depleted. No one wants that.

As our Into the Fire participants sat on the beach for the final hours of the surf retreat, Gary and I ran to greet them like a group of Baywatch lifeguards carrying the inflatable unicorn that Emma had wished into existence.

I told the whole story, starting where we offered to honor requests to create delight and how none but Emma asked for anything, and she only did after she was encouraged, nudged, or pushed. (I'm not sure which. I am rather persistent.) I asked how often we miss opportunities to create joy and meaning simply because we don't ask for what we want (especially if it seems silly or indulgent) or worse, we don't ask for anything at all?

Emma and I threw ourselves onto the inflatable unicorn to catch a few waves before the lifeguards kindly asked us to remove our toy from the ocean. Apparently, it wasn't safe to surf a unicorn near surfboards and swimmers—maybe not safe, but totally spectacular, and I loved every ridiculous minute!

Perhaps the most amazing breakthrough moment of the retreat was seeing Emma realize that she could have anything she wanted and, by extension, so could we all.

ZUMA MEANS ABUNDANCE

I think one of the lessons about surfing is how to operate in the present. That's really what the foundation of the entire surfing experience is. – from the movie *A Brokedown Melody*

WHEN WE LOST INDY SO SUDDENLY, I heard these words at the end of a song, and it reminded me that the only time we have is NOW. Not yesterday, not tomorrow, not even five minutes in the future. We get now, as beautiful and as broken as it is. This is why I surf. It is my practice to learn how to be with exactly what is in each moment, whether I'm riding a wave or caught under one.

With our dear Indy gone, Rafe asked me to consider the possibility of welcoming a new companion to our family, whenever I was ready. I sat at home with our six-year-old Ruby and realized, while I might learn to be okay without a second dog, she needed one. He was the yang to her yin.

What is the right time? Is there such a thing?

Committed to staying open to love, I made a call, and Ruby and I took an adventure back out to Fillmore to visit our friends at Dobies and Little Paws Rescue. On the drive, a dog-loving colleague of mine called me to offer her condolences. "Indy will send you a message," she told me with an intuitive confidence I needed to believe, and minutes later I heard a song that if Indy could have dedicated to me, he would have. Of course, it was a love song by Ed Sheerhan called "Tenerife Sea."

> *And should this be the last thing I see*
> *I want you to know it's enough for me*
> *'Cause all that you are is all that I'll ever need*
> *I'm so in love, so in love*
> *So in love, so in love*

I don't know that I've cried as many tears in my life as I did in the month we lost Papi then, three weeks later, my sweet Indy.

And then I thought if there were another dog to join our family, he'd have a beach name, maybe something from Hawaii. I recalled something Rafe had shared with me: Zuma is the Chumash word meaning abundance. When I think of Indy, I never want to think of how short his life was but rather how much love was packed into his five years. I want to remember his abundance. Zuma. Zuma is where I surf. Zuma is sacred to me.

There is no need to postpone happiness. In the many complexities of life, you can mourn and grieve and be delighted at the same exact time. We are big enough for all our emotions, not only the ones that hang out at the front of the line.

We met many dogs that weren't the right fit for us and one that was a brown dog who licked me on the elbow like Indy would, who looked like him and not like him at all. His name was Rebel, but now he's called Zuma. He is a joy.

Sometimes, I call Zuma Indy by mistake. It's a high compliment.

LIFE LESSONS FROM A SEPHORA MAKEOVER

FOR A LONG, LONG TIME, I prided myself on knowing a lot. Knowing things, being smart, getting things right, etc. were a big part of my identity and how I felt I was valued and valuable. Plus, I was awesome at Trivial Pursuit and hardly ever forgot a name. Now, I'm happy and humbled to acknowledge when I don't know.

Until one afternoon at Sephora, I didn't know about eye shadow primer, glitter glue, or natural looking (and exquisite) lashes. But look at what happens when you hand yourself over to a pro! We don't know what we don't know, and if we're being honest, what we **do** know pales in comparison to the vast mysteries of life. Most of what we "know" is an interpretation, at best.

One spring before the Tony Awards, Ellie and I saw the best-nominated shows on Broadway. I was so taken in by one of the performances, I ended up with an empathy hangover. It obviously wasn't the first time I'd taken on outside emotions as my own, but it was one of the first times I noticed the impact and could connect my feelings to *someone else's experience*.

THERE'S GOT TO BE A BETTER WAY

Why was I having all the feelings? Because I felt them and didn't separate myself from them. I reached out to my spiritual mechanic magical energy maven Megan for guidance. We had been working on learning how to develop an understanding of my energy sensitivities along with learning tools to stay grounded, connected, on purpose, and productive.

She tells me things, and I'm in awe. It's like discovering surfing or seeing a baby smile. For instance, in our last session when I'd shared some challenges I was sensitive to, she reminded me that energy can be like a hose that gets kinked. Our job is to stay as clear as possible to stay in flow. Sounds simple, but isn't necessarily easy…much like applying false eyelashes.

Bottom line: you've got to do the work. What does that mean on a practical level? You already know this, and I'm going to write it out anyway.

(1) If you need therapy, get therapy. There is absolutely ZERO shame asking for help. I've had wonderful therapists in my life who've helped me recover from really dark places and old patterns. Like coaches, a good therapist will help you see what you couldn't otherwise see and to heal and create new and healthy ways of coping and living.

(2) Take care of yourself. Get the sleep you need. Move your body often. Nourish yourself well. Supplement where needed. The more empathic you are, the more you need to support your adrenal system to manage the unseen stresses (and accompanying cortisol spikes) you are prone to take on without noticing. Allow yourself to rest

at the beginning of a cold, not when it's full blown and you're out of commission. Pay attention to your body. Listen to what she tells you. Follow her lead.

(3) Expand your self-awareness and self-concept. Be a curiously fascinated and unattached student of your own life's experience. Be willing to see differently. Allow your own evolution, and give yourself a bunch of high fives and gold stars for how far you've come! Look at you go! You might be able to do this on your own, but we often struggle to see the complete picture of ourselves from within the frame. Seek out people (coaches, mentors, friends) who see you in the best ways and the way you want to see yourself. Be honest, be gentle, and be compassionate. It can be hard to be you sometimes. I feel you.

It's easy to be a powerhouse, but without integration, having access to all that power and not managing it through your own sensitivity makes you more likely to melt down. The more power, the bigger the potential for nuclear disaster. No one wants that, especially not you.

In the rest of the world, it might feel like we have to explain being sensitive, empathic, intuitive, or whatever your particular brand of genius is. Not here, my friends. Not on this boat. Not on my watch.

LET'S COLOR AND GO IN THE OCEAN

IN THE SPRING OF 2018, I met the Good Doctor. She was referred to me by one of my amazing clients, and we got on a call to explore working together.

New to coaching, she shared some obstacles in her work and how she felt limited in her approach to addressing them. She wanted to change and heard I might be able to help.

We spoke about how I work, my leadership philosophy, the experiential approach, and then played together with the application of my theories into the practicalities of her unique situation. By the end of the conversation, I'd helped her remember what she loved most. I gave her homework and guidance on how to bring that sense of fun and lightness into a project she was dreading. She messaged me the next day to tell me that she tried what I suggested, and it worked!

I hadn't looked at the Good Doctor's online résumé until after we spoke. I had no idea how much she had achieved or accomplished in her life. It was stunning to see and then humbling to realize what I'd offered in service to one of the world's leading experts.

As I shared this experience with Rafe, I explained that I'd basically told this genius to have fun, color, and go in the ocean and, almost instantaneously, she found the ability to find a better way.

It took me awhile to arrive here, but now it's who I am.

TRAUMA BRAIN, PART 3

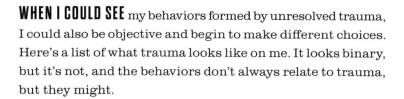

WHEN I COULD SEE my behaviors formed by unresolved trauma, I could also be objective and begin to make different choices. Here's a list of what trauma looks like on me. It looks binary, but it's not, and the behaviors don't always relate to trauma, but they might.

Trauma Brain	Wise, Empowered Mind
Avoiding conflict	Being clear, communicative, and assertive
Overcomplicating	Taking a pause, asking questions, being curious, there is no "right" answer
Isolating, withdrawing, numbing	Asking for help, being honest and vulnerable
Anticipating everyone's needs, self-care comes last	Knowing that taking care of myself makes it easier to take care of others

Drama, attention-seeking behaviors	Healthy self-awareness
Keeping secrets	Trusting people to hear my stories
Forced independence	Receiving help (even imperfect)
Catastrophizing	Acknowledging my tendency to turn normal events into potential catastrophic events, looking for easier solutions and multiple perspectives
Perfectionism	High standards + resilience, maintaining a growth mindset, and always having room to improve
Accommodating	Advocating
Reactive	Responsive
Victim	Survivor
I am responsible for everything!	I am responsible for myself.
Controlling	Allowing

| Recycling the past, looking for answers | Accepting the past, connecting to feelings, letting go |

Healing is simple but not easy.

If you recognize yourself among the millions who have survived adverse childhood experiences, know that you are not alone. It's really hard. I hope you find an amazing therapist, psychologist, social worker, rabbi, pastor, coach, counselor, or healer who can help you find your way back home. (I think I've worked with at least one of each. You'll forgive me if I've left some out. It's been quite a long journey.)

What's wrong with me?

When you ask this question directly and indirectly your whole life, you always find answers. One day, I stopped asking. After a lifetime seeking, I found the most unexpected answer: *nothing* was wrong with me. Not one goddamned thing.

HOME

HOME IS YOU. Home is knowing you have value and worth simply because you exist. Home is being able to distinguish the negative voices, circumstances, and stories of your life from the truth of who you are, that delightful presence with your unique DNA sequence who is more than the sum of their parts—or any list of accomplishments.

If you don't yet know that you are okay, that you are here, and that your life has meaning because you're living it, please ask for help and don't stop. Take as long as you need. You matter.

The path of healing—like life—is long and crooked with many detours. Somehow, despite the unfortunate events of my childhood, I've turned out to be quite extraordinary. I always knew there had to be a better way, and it started with me learning to see myself differently.

There's no magic formula to creating, living, and leading your best life, but I've learned one thing to be true above all else: you have to love the sound of your inner voice. You don't need more information, you need to learn how to listen to yourself.

As author Derek Sivers said, "If more information were the answer, we'd all be billionaires with perfect abs."

Know yourself. Only you can find the way. I always wished someone had given me a guidebook to navigate life. Instead, I ended up writing my own.

MY VILLAGE: ACKNOWLEDGMENTS

I take a village.

I have been inspired by writers who wrote strong women characters and told stories that guided me as I grew up. Erma Bombeck, Carolyn Keene, Louisa May Alcott, Laura Ingalls Wilder, Judy Blume, Agatha Christie, Danielle Steel, Lena Dunham, Jenny Lawson, Elizabeth Gilbert, Brené Brown, Cheryl Strayed, and Oprah Winfrey are my honorary aunties.

I have been supported to grow personally, professionally, and spiritually by great humans, including the best bosses I ever had, Tod Lipka and Kevin Honeycutt. Dr. Donn Warshow, David Darst, Linda Moore are among a tribe of giants who have helped me to know and love myself exactly as I am and so much more.

I love you to the moon and back, my soul siblings: wonder twin, co-founder + bfbp forever, Gary Mahler; Rose Red to my Snow White, Sweet Caroline Carrie Kish; woman of faith Beth Strear; and my rockstar Alumni Scholar sisters Jama and Melissa. ITF is my ohana, most especially Emma Holmes (aka Emmacorn) who wears a wetsuit like a dolphin wears its skin.

THERE'S GOT TO BE A BETTER WAY

Our Wrong Turn Ranch family, Angi, Seth, and Nina, are the best horse people you will ever know. My family of origin and family by marriage are my rocks: Daddy, William Aric Israel (of blessed memory), Ryan, Mom and Terry, Grammi and Papi (of blessed memory), partners in mischief Auntie Banana and C-Note.

I am grateful for every person who has ever told me, "I love your writing, you should write a book." So much love to all the people who have opened their hearts and lives to me and have given me the honor of serving as their coach. My early readers, thank you for the great gift of telling me how you hear my voice. This book is better because of you. Super special thanks to Chris Ovens for our weekly calls that had both nothing and everything to do with helping me see this project to completion. Amanda Johnson, you are a dream come true. When I asked for an editor who, like Mary Poppins, is practically perfect in every way, you magically appeared. How awesome is that?!

אני לדודי ודודי לי

I am my beloved's and my beloved is mine/Ani L'Dodi V'Dodi Li. To Rafe who has given me life and infinite reasons and ways to live, love, and create. My beautiful and perfect Jake and Ellie, the depths to which I love you have made me whole.

RESOURCES

Books That Have Made an Impact

The Gifts of Imperfection, Dr. Brené Brown

Man's Search for Meaning, Viktor Frankl

Rework, Jason Fried and David Heinemeier Hansson

The Inner Game of Stress, W. Timothy Gallwey

Big Magic, Elizabeth Gilbert

West of Jesus: Surfing, Science and the Origins of Belief, Steven Kotler

Let's Pretend This Never Happened, Jenny Lawson

Hamilton: The Revolution, Lin-Manuel Miranda, Jeremy McCarter

Pollyanna, Eleanor H. Porter

The Empath's Survival Guide, Judith Orloff, M.D.

Presence, Peter Senge, C. Otto Scharmer, Joseph Jaworsky, Betty Sue Flowers

The Surrender Experiment, Michael A. Singer

Tiny Beautiful Things: Advice on Love and Life from Dear Sugar, Cheryl Strayed

Never Split the Difference: Negotiating as if Your Life Depended on It, Chris Voss

Kanako's Into the Fire Cookies

Handmade and served at the Into the Fire Surf Retreats in Malibu

Recipe makes approximately 18-20 cookies
Preheat oven to 375 degrees F

Ingredients:

1 cup flour (use a blend: 1/3 cup organic sprouted spelt flour, 1/3 cup teff flour, 1/3 cup organic brown rice flour or quinoa flakes)

2 tbsp ground flax

1/8 tsp sea or Himalayan salt

1/4 tsp aluminum free baking soda

1/2 tsp baking powder

1 tsp organic vanilla extract

1 organic egg

2/3 cup coconut sugar

1/2 cup organic butter or ghee (or 1/4 cup coconut oil + 1/4 cup organic butter/ ghee)

3/4 cup organic unsweetened shredded coconut

1 cup organic rolled oats

2 tbsp mini chocolate chips

Handful of chocolate chunks (optional)

Combine flour, salt, baking soda, flax, and baking powder in bowl. In separate bowl or food processor mix sugar and butter (or alternative combo) until blended. Add egg and vanilla and mix. Add flour mixture, mix again. Next, combine coconut and mix. Add rolled oats and mix. Last add chocolate chips.

Using a measuring tablespoon, scoop out cookie dough, form dough into ball and place on parchment lined baking sheet. Wet a fork with water and flatten cookie ball slightly. Insert optional chocolate chunk. Place in oven 11-13 minutes or until toasty brown.

Cool completely so cookies can set. Enjoy!

ABOUT THE AUTHOR

KAREN PERY, MA, CPCC, is a certified executive coach with a focus on leadership development. Creating and leading fun and immersive retreats, programs, and experiences since 1987, she can be found teaching leaders to find their better way through surfing in Hawaii, getting  feedback from horses in Santa Barbara wine country, and via her blogs, newsletters, and private sessions.

Karen and Rafe Pery split their time between Los Angeles and Santa Ynez, California with their teenagers Jake and Ellie, dogs Ruby and Zuma, a small flock of chickens, a herd of rescued horses, and two donkeys.

Discover more at karenpery.com.

Made in the USA
Middletown, DE
04 January 2019